MW00652224

THIS PAGE INTENTIONALLY LEFT BLANK

THIS PAGE INTENTIONALLY LEFT BLANK

Franz Lehár
Die Lustige Witwe
(THE MERRY WIDOW)

OPERETTA STUDY GUIDE with LIBRETTO

OPERA CLASSICS LIBRARY™ SERIES

Edited by Burton D. Fisher
Principal lecturer, *Opera Journeys Lecture Series*

Opera Journeys™ Publishing / Boca Raton, Florida

All musical notations contained herein are original transcriptions
by Opera Journeys Publishing.

WEB SITE: www.operajourneys.com   E MAIL: operaj@bellsouth.net

Franz Lehár — Die Lustige Witwe   *Page 5*

Contents

Opera Journeys™ *Mini Guide Series*

Opera Classics Library™ *Series*

Opera Journeys™ *Libretto Series*

A History of Opera:
Milestones and Metamorphoses

Mozart's Da Ponte Operas

PUCCINI COMPANION

Verdi Companion: 27 Opera Study Guide

Over 125 GUIDES & LIBRETTI AVAILABLE: Print or Ebook

•The Abduction from the Seraglio •Adriana Lecouvreur •L'Africaine •Aida
•Andrea Chénier •Anna Bolena •Ariadne auf Naxos •Armida •Attila
•The Ballad of Baby Doe •The Barber of Seville •Duke Bluebeard's Castle
•La Bohème •Boris Godunov •Candide •Capriccio •Carmen
•Cavalleria Rusticana •Cendrillon •La Cenerentola •La Clemenza di Tito
•Le Comte Ory •Così fan tutte •The Crucible •La Damnation de Faust
•The Death of Klinghoffer •Doctor Atomic •Don Carlo •Don Giovanni
•Don Pasquale •La Donna del Lago •The Elixir of Love •Elektra •Ernani
•Eugene Onegin •Exploring Wagner's Ring •Falstaff •La Fanciulla del West
•Faust •La Fille du Régiment •Fidelio •Die Fledermaus •The Flying Dutchman
•Die Frau ohne Schatten •Der Freischütz •Gianni Schicchi •La Gioconda
•Hamlet •Hansel and Gretel •Henry VIII •Iolanta •L'Italiana in Algeri
•Les Huguenots •Iphigénie en Tauride •Julius Caesar •Lakmé •Lohengrin
•Lucia di Lammermoor •Macbeth •Madama Butterfly •The Magic Flute
•The Makropolis Case •Manon •Manon Lescaut •Maria Stuarda
•The Marriage of Figaro •A Masked Ball •Die Meistersinger •The Mikado
•Nabucco •Nixon in China •Norma •Of Mice and Men •Orfeo ed Euridice
•Otello •I Pagliacci •Parsifal •The Pearl Fishers •Pelléas et Mélisande
•Porgy and Bess •Prince Igor •I Puritani •The Queen of Spades
•The Rake's Progress •The Rape of Lucretia •The Rhinegold •Rigoletto
•The Ring of the Nibelung •Roberto Devereaux •Rodalinda •Roméo et Juliette
•La Rondine •Der Rosenkavalier •Rusalka •Salome •Samson and Delilah
•Show Boat •Siegfried •Simon Boccanegra •La Sonnambula •Suor Angelica
•Susannah •Il Tabarro •The Tales of Hoffmann •Tannhäuser •Thaïs •Tosca
•La Traviata •Tristan and Isolde •Il Trittico •Les Troyens •Il Trovatore
•Turandot •The Valkyrie •Werther •West Side Story •Wozzeck

WWW.OPERAJOURNEYS.COM

a Prelude....

OPERA CLASSICS LIBRARY's

Die Lustige Witwe

STUDY GUIDE WITH LIBRETTO

Franz Lehár is primarily renowned as the second generation of the Viennese operetta tradition; *Die Lustige Witwe* represents the genre at its peak of romantic elegance, which is captured through Lehár's luscious melodies, charming style, and expert craftsmanship.

With *Die Lustige Witwe*, Lehár brought Viennese operetta into the twentieth century; it served to inaugurate the genre's silver age.

The Opera Journeys' text contains a *Brief Story Synopsis, Principal Characters,* a *Story Narrative with Music Highlight Examples,* and Burton D. Fisher's insightful and in depth *Commentary and Analysis.* In addition, the text includes a *Dictionary of Opera and Musical Terms.*

The *Libretto* provides a new translation of German to English, side-by-side..

The opera art form represents a "Gesamtkunstwerk" that captures many artistic expressions: theatrical drama, music, scenery, poetry, dance, and singing.

Die Lustige Witwe provides a delightful theatrical experience with music that can profoundly impact one's sensibilities.

Burton D. Fisher
Editor
OPERA CLASSICS LIBRARY

Die Lustige Witwe
(THE MERRY WIDOW)

Operetta in German in three acts

Music
by
Franz Lehár

Libretto by Viktor Léon and Leo Stein,
from the play *L'attaché d'ambassade* (1861)
by Henri Meilhac
In the German translation,
Der Gesandschafts Attaché (1862)
by Alexander Bergen

Premiere: Vienna, December 1905

Commentary and Analysis

Austro-Hungarian composer Franz Lehár (1870 — 1948) endowed the operetta genre with energy and vitality with *Die Lustige Witwe* ("The Merry Widow"), a singular masterpiece that achieved overwhelming acclaim since its 1905 premiere and has remained a perennial favorite of the international lyric theater.

Lehár inherited his musical genes from his father, a military bandmaster, composer of dances and marches, and a musician in the orchestra of Vienna's Theater an der Wien. At the age of 12, young Lehár demonstrated exceptional talent as a violinist; after receiving encouragement from Antonin Dvorak, he entered the Prague Conservatory where he continued studies in violin, theory, harmony, and composition.

At 18, Lehár became a violinist in a provincial theater orchestra. He was later called into the military where he played in military bands alongside his father and Leo Fall (1873 — 1925), an Austrian who was later to become an operetta composer.

In 1902, at the age of 32, Lehár left military service and began conducting and composing. His early works included the operetta *Kukuschka* (1896); the popular waltz *Gold und Silber* (1902); and the operettas, *Wiener Frauen* (originally entitled *Der Klavierstimmer*), *Der Rastelbinder* (The Tinker), *Der Göttergatte*, and *Die Juxheirat* (1904). Lehár also received acclaim for *Der Graf von Luxemburg* (1909) and *Zigeunerliebe* (1910), the latter a magnificent blend of melancholy and fantasy. The operetta *Eva* (1911) followed the trend toward realism with a scenario that featured a factory girl involved in conflicting social relationships; and *Endlich Allein* (1914), its leading protagonists alone on a mountaintop.

Operetta — a form of lyric theater — is a diminutive of "opera": "opérette" in French; "Operett" in German; "opereta" in Spanish — musical storytelling in which the drama is realized and intensified through deeds of music. Traditionally, operetta integrates popular subjects and styles that possess less intensity in its drama and music. As such, the term "operetta" has commonly been applied as a generic that describes musical theater works that represent a derivative of opera — shorter, less ambitious works that contain much spoken dialogue.

By the 1870s, Vienna had become the artistic and cultural center of the Hapsburg Empire, but Austrians were becoming xenophobic after they realized that a vast number of their musical theater works were imported — in particular, the French operettes, or opere bouffes, of Jacques Offenbach, the father of the operetta genre.

Viennese theatrical impressarios were determined to incorporate an Austrian ethos in its lyric theater works. They turned to Johann Strauss Jr., the son of the "waltz king" who they envisioned as the rescuer of Austria's musical theater; Strauss was a genius with the stature and talent to meet the formidable task of composing music that captured the Austrian cultural soul. Strauss was further encouraged to meet the challenge by his wife, the singer Jetty Treffz, who persuaded him to resign as 'Hofballmusikdirektor' and concentrate all of his efforts on composing for the lyric theater; Strauss ceded the direction of the family orchestra to Eduard, his only surviving brother.

Strauss completed a host of Viennese operettas, reaching the pinnacle of his successes with *Der Karneval in Rom* ('The Carnival in Rome') (1873); *Die Fledermaus* ('The Bat') (1874); and *Der Zigeunerbaron* ('The Gypsy Baron') (1885), the latter's second-act love duet considered by many to portray the quintessence of the Viennese romantic spirit.

Nevertheless, _Die Fledermaus_ has been universally acclaimed as Strauss's tour de force, an ingenious work whose text and music magnificently capture the vivacious romantic and sentimental spirit of late nineteenth-century Vienna.

Franz Lehár became the heir to the Strauss operetta legacy: _Die Lustige Witwe_ (1905) heralded a new era for Viennese operetta that would eventually be emulated by composer-disciples such as Leo Fall; Oscar Strauss (1870 — 1954); and Emmerich Kálmán (1882 — 1953).

The end of World War I signaled the end of the Austro-Hungarian Empire — and also the diminishing popularity of operetta. To rejuvenate his operettas, Lehár incorporated American musical idioms into his music scores: blues, foxtrots, tangos, and shimmies. But his attempt at integrating foreign styles into his scores backfired; Lehár's popularity became a victim of post-war Austrian xenophobia.

Nevertheless, Lehár experienced a new surge of success from his association with the internationally popular tenor, Richard Tauber (1892 —1948). Earlier, Tauber had achieved acclaim for his portrayal of Tamino in Mozart's _Die Zauberflöte;_ Belmonte in _The Abduction from the Seraglio;_ and Don Ottavio in _Don Giovanni_. As the 1920s unfolded, Tauber shifted the focus of his career to operetta.

After he befriended Lehár, the composer dutifully provided him with virile and forceful tenor roles — known as "Tauber-Lied": operettas such as _Paganini_ (1925); _Der Zarewitsch_ (1927); and _Friederike_ (1928), the latter featuring Tauber in the role of Goethe. Hallmark songs emanated from the Lehar-Tauber collaboration, such as " Dein ist mein ganzes Herz" from Lehar's widely popular _Das Land des Lächelns_ (1929), and "O Mädchen, mein Mädchen" from _Friederike._

Like Jacques Offenbach, and Johann Strauss Jr., his operetta predecessors, Lehár yearned to compose a serious opera: _Giuditta_ (1934) became his singular serious work, which was produced by the Vienna Staatsoper in 1934 and featured Richard Tauber and Jarmila Novotna in its leading roles.

In later life, Lehár concentrated on preserving the lucrative rights to his stage works; he eventually acquired the rights to all of his works from their respective publishers, with the notable exception of _Die Lustige Witwe_. Nevertheless, the _Witwe_'s phenomenal and enduring success and revenues from stage and music royalties very quickly made Lehár rich and famous.

In 1938, after the Nazis annexed Austria, and the 68-year-old Lehár found himself ensconced in Vienna and Bad Ischl. Like so many German artists of the time, Lehár faced the paradox of confronting the relationship between art and politics; he believed that art superseded politics and that the Nazi's had disgraced German honor. But survival during wartime demanded that he become a compliant artist. As a result, the Nazis supported his works and considered him one of their prized "Aryan" composers.

Lehár protested as he sadly witnessed many friends and collaborators disappearing to concentration camps, an outcry that was both weak and futile. During the terror of the Second World War, Vienna was hardly the carefree operetta capital that had highlighted it past. Jewish artists such as Mizzi Güther, the original Hanna of _Die Lustige Witwe,_ was relegated to playing small dowager roles on Viennese operetta stages; the first Danilo, Louis Treumann, was deported to the "model" concentration camp at Theresienstadt where he died in 1942.

Lehár claimed to be apolitical and therefore shared many of the same dilemmas as internationally renowned composer Richard Strauss. Lehár did everything possible to protect his Jewish wife; Strauss's son Franz was married to Alice Graf, a Jewish woman — as such, Strauss's daughter-in-law was the mother of two Jewish grandchildren. It has been speculated that Strauss — and perhaps Lehár — made a bargain with the Nazis that effectively exchanged silence for family protection.

During the war, Lehár continued to conduct in Vienna and Berlin and promoted his popular lyric theater works at important German and Austrian theaters; he reputedly overcame the Third Reich's sensitivity to the huge royalties he was collecting from *Die Lustige Witwe* performances in allied cities.

Hitler was a passionate admirer of *Die Lustige Witwe*, the operetta's Vienna-Paris excesses obviously appealing to him — a remarkable anomaly considering the historical perspective and the realization that both its librettists — and Lehár's wife — were Jews.

Before or after the Nazis, no one of Strauss's operas — or Lehár's operettas — contained a political subtext or underlying ideological message. With the clarity of historical hindsight, it would be presumptuous to stand in judgment of the politics of these artists, but in truth, they were artists struggling for survival in a world that crossed the line into insanity and therefore, for practical purposes, they invoked silence as a means of protecting their families — Strauss and Lehár were neither heroes nor martyrs.

Lehár died in 1946. His villa at Bad Ischl is now a Lehár museum.

Over the course of some 20 years, the French writers Henri Meilhac (1831—1897) and Ludovic Halévy (1834 — 1908) had collaborated on numerous plays and librettos; their most enduring works were those written for Offenbach, and adapted Mérimée's novella for Bizet's *Carmen*. Meilhac was renowned for his imagination in developing uninhibited comic verve and wit in the creation of brazen parodies and hilarious satires; Halévy was a craftsman noted for his talent in developing the scenarios and the dramatic framework.

French plays, comedies and satires were traditionally viewed with favor and esteem by the Austrian theater public: Meilhac's comedy, *L'Attaché d'Ambassade*, had originally been produced at the Variétés in 1861 and had achieved favorable acclaim when it was produced in Vienna.

Stein (1861 — 1921) was a prolific writer of operetta librettos who had earlier collaborated with Victor Léon (1858 — 1940) on Lehár's *Wiener Blut* (1899), a pastiche of Johann Strauss Jr. melodies that had achieved spectacular success. It was Stein who proposed the idea of transforming Meilhac's *L'Attaché* into an operetta for Lehár. However, many of the names in Meilhac's *L'Attaché* were changed to avoid the association with a German principality — the fictitious Balkan state of "Pontevedro" resolved the issue.

Lehár's *Die Lustige Witwe* was composed during a period of harmonic adventurism in music: Debussy's Impressionism created visual images through deeds of music; Richard Strauss's shock operas, *Salome* (1905) and *Elektra* (1909), attempted to translate subconscious emotive states into the musical language; and Arnold Schoenberg's atonalism avoided harmonic tonal centers or key relationships. Nevertheless, Lehár remained steadfast in composing tonal music in diatonic, traditional harmonies.

Waltzes were strongly identified with Vienna during the nineteenth and early twentiethcenturies; the oeuvre of Johann Strauss and his family continued to dominate nineteenth century operetta scores. Franz Lehár became the heir to the Strauss Viennese waltz traditions, providing society's music for song and dance up until the advent of World War I.

Die Lustige Witwe and its lush and sentimental waltzes have become a metaphor for the glamorous "Belle Epoque" preceding World War I, its waltzes symbolizing a carefree world indulging in the pursuit of pleasure, gaiety, and abandon.

*D*ie *Lustige Witwe* premiered on Dec. 30, 1905; it was immediately acclaimed, and almost overnight all of Vienna was buying the sheet music of the operetta's hit tunes. Lehár's operetta rejuvenated the Viennese genre; it became the rage internationally with a London production that ran for 778 performances, and performances in the colonies of Rangoon and Calcutta.

In the United States, the operetta became the center of a frenzy for the young evolving film industry. MGM acquired the rights to make film versions. In 1925, Erich von Stroheim produced the operetta for film, modifying the original story and creating the heroine "Sally," an American chorus girl who eventually became the "merry widow" of the title — Mae Murray and John Gilbert were the film's lovers. In 1934, Ernst Lubitsch's "The Lady Dances" represented a faithful film version of the original story and became the first sound version of the operetta, but strangely excluded much of Lehár's music even though it featured Jeanette MacDonald and Maurice Chevalier — ideal portrayers of "Sonia" and "Danilo" Lana Turner and Fernando Lamas were far less ideal lovers in Curtis Bernhardt's 1952 film. Decades later, a new production directed by Ingmar Bergman starred Barbra Streisand, but it came to naught.

Die Lustige Witwe remains high on the list of the most performed operettas; it has variously been translated, recorded, broadcast, televised, and has provided inspiration for ballet as well as ice skating choreography. In 1943, Marta Eggerth and Jan Kiepura enjoyed a Broadway revival at the Majestic Theater, and in 1964 it opened the Richard Rogers Music Theater in Lincoln Center with Patrice Munsel in the title role. Countless opera stars have been drawn to the title role: Maria Jeritza, Kirsten Flagstad, Beverly Sills, and Joan Sutherland, the latter establishing the widow as one of her late career roles, in which she relished the opportunity it provided to indulge her hearty sense of humor.

*D*ie *Lustige Witwe* introduced a strange theatrical marriage of stylized Viennese waltz tunes together with imitations of the Parisian cancan dances. Like Lehár's Viennese predecessor, Johann Strauss Jr., the waltz was the centerpiece of the operetta; but in comparison, Lehár's waltzes seem to contain more tenderness, more swaying, and certainly more sensuality. But charm remains the main ingredient of Lehár's more sentimental Viennese operetta; although at times he introduced satire into his scenarios, social commentary is rare.

Lehár's orchestrations are noteworthy and no doubt represent the composer's homage to his contemporaries, such as Dvorak, Debussy, Puccini, and Richard Strauss. In addition,

Lehár was exceptional in capturing the idioms of local color: Slavic rhythms in *Der Rastelbinder;* Balkan flavor in *Die Lustige Witwe;* Polish folk idiom in *Die Blaue Mazue*; Spanish in *Frasquita;* Russian in *Der Zarewirtsch;* and the oriental in *Das Land das Lächelns.*

Lehár was an accomplished violinist who seized every opportunity for exhibitionist violin solos, which he brilliantly incorporated in the operettas *Zigeinerliebe, Die Blaue Mazur* and *Paganini.* The solo violin is always a feature that pervades and heightens the sensuousness of Lehár's love-scenes, similar to the effect of Johann Strauss's romantic waltzes.

Many of Lehár's operettas were transplanted to England and the United States under their English titles: *The Man with Three Wives* (1908); *The Count of Luxembourg* (1909); *Gypsy Love* (1910); *The Land of Smiles* (1923). At first, the American musical theater had to compete with European-style operetta. Although Broadway eventually became the victor, most Viennese operettas remain in the contemporary musical theater because they generate musical and emotional nostalgia —a tenacious hold on popular affections that had been continued in American operettas, such as Rudolf Friml's *Rose Marie* (1924), and Sigmund Romberg's *The Desert Song* (1926).

Lehár's predecessor, Johann Strauss Jr., established the model for the Viennese operetta genre through his expert blend of charm and craft, all patently evident in *Die Fledermaus* (1874), a seemingly eternal classic. Lehár is primarily renowned as the second generation of the Viennese operetta tradition, *Die Lustige Witwe* representing the genre at its peak of romantic elegance, which is captured through Lehár's luscious melodies, charming style, and expert craftsmanship.

With *Die Lustige Witwe*, Lehár brought Viennese operetta into the twentieth century and served to inaugurate the genre's silver age.

Principal Characters in Die Lustige Witwe

Hanna Glawari, a rich widow	Soprano
Count Danilo Danilovitsch, First Secretary of the embassy, Hanna's former lover	Tenor or Baritone
Baron Mirko Zeta, the Pontevedrian Ambassador	Baritone
Valencienne, Baron Zeta's wife	Soprano
Camille, Count de Rosillon, French attaché to the embassy, and admirer of the Valencienne	Tenor
Njegus, Embassy Secretary	Spoken
Kromow, Pontevedrian Embassy advisor	Baritone
Olga, Kromow's wife	Mezzo soprano
Bogdanovitch, Pontevedrian military attaché	Baritone
Sylviane, Bogdanovitch's wife	Soprano
Raoul de St. Brioche, French diplomat	Baritone
Vicomte Cascada, French	Baritone
Pritschitsch, a retired Pontevedrian colonel	Baritone
Praskowia, Pritschitsch's wife	Mezzo soprano

Parisians, Pontevedrians, musicians and servants

TIME: Late nineteenth century
PLACE: Paris

Brief Story Synopsis

The recently widowed Hanna Glawari has become heir to a fortune. It is essential for the survival of the tiny country of Pontevedro that she marry a Pontevedrian rather than a foreigner, thus keeping her financial assets in the country.

In Paris, Baron Zeta, the Pontevedrian Ambassador, orders his high-living attaché Count Danilo to serve his fatherland by marrying Hanna. In the past, Hanna and Danilo had been in love, but their romance ended after Danilo's uncle forbid him to marry a woman of such poor financial and social status.

The entire plot of *Die Lustige Witwe* involves Baron Zeta's intrigues to reunite the embittered lovers, Hanna and Danilo, and thus save Pontevedro from bankruptcy.

Story Narrative and Music Highlight Examples

Act I: Embassy of Pontevedro in Paris

The poverty-stricken principality of Pontevedro is celebrating the birthday of its sovereign, the Grand Duke. The honored guest at the festivities is Hanna Glawari, a recent widow, who has just inherited a considerable fortune from her late husband. Baron Zeta, the Pontevedrian ambassador, is scheming to ensure that Hanna will keep her fortune in Pontevedro, thus saving the country from bankruptcy.

Zeta has chosen Count Danilo Danilovitsch, the first secretary of the embassy, to perform his patriotic duty and marry the widow. But at the moment, Danilo must be fetched from Maxim's, his favorite cabaret.

"Da geh'ich zu Maxim, dort bin ich sehr intim" ("Then I go off to Maxim's, there I am very familiar")

Years ago, Danilo and Hanna were lovers, but Danilo's uncle ended their romance because Hanna was a woman of poor means and unacceptable social status. Hanna is a now a wealthy widow; if Danilo pursues her, she would no doubt condemn him as a fortune-seeker. Danilo refuses Zeta's order to court Hanna.

Meanwhile, Zeta's wife Valencienne has been flirting with Count Camille de Rosillon, the French attaché to the embassy; he has written "I love you" on her fan. Valencienne attempts to shrug off Camille's advances by proclaiming that she is a respectable wife. Valencienne has misplaced the incriminating fan.

As the "Ladies Choice" waltz begins, Hanna becomes swarmed with hopeful dancing partners. Valencienne suggests that Camille dance with Hanna, privately hoping that the Frenchman would marry the widow and cease pursing Valencienne herself.

Danilo arrives with a bevy of young women, a ploy to evade being chosen by Hanna as her waltz partner. But Hanna does choose Danilo for the dance, the one man who had totally ignored her. Danilo declines Hanna's offer but announces that he will sell his dance opportunity with Hanna for ten thousand francs and give the proceeds to charity.

After much resistance, Hanna succeeds in inviting Danilo to dance with her.

The couple fall into eachother's arms and dance a sensuous waltz.

"Ballsirenenwalzer" ("Sirens of the Ball")
"O kommet doch, o kommt, ihr Ballsirenen, folgt den süssen Walzertönen"
("Oh come, o come, you ball-lovers, follow the sweet waltz tunes")

Act II: Hanna Glawari's villa, the following day

Hanna hosts a party at her villa. She entertains guests by singing an old Pontevedrian song: Vilja, a tale of a forest nymph who took her life after her lover's betrayal.

"Vilja, o Vilja, du Waldmägdelein" ("Vilja, o Vilja, maid of the woods")

That evening, Camille and Valencienne meet in the garden. Valencienne insists that they must part. Camille discoveres Valencienne's fan which was accidentally left behind and begs her to give it to him as a keepsake. Valencienne writes on the fan, "I am a respectable wife" — a rejoinder to Camille having written, "I love you." Camille persuades Valencienne to join him in the pavilion so for a private farewell.

Njegus, an embassy employee, sees two people in the pavilion; he locks the door and hurriedly reports to Zeta that Camille and a lady are in the pavilion. Zeta resorts to spying on them. He peeps through a keyhole and to his horror, recognizes his wife.

To avoid a scandal, Njegus arranges for Hanna to change places with Valencienne. Camille emerges from the pavilion with Hanna; Camille expresses his passionate love to the woman — but this time the recipient of his passion is Hanna.

Zeta becomes distraught at the thought of Pontevedro losing Hanna's millions. Simultaneously, Danilo cannot disguise his disgust at the turn of events.

Hanna further provokes Danilo's fury by vowing to marry Camille and live in Parisian luxury. Danilo expesses his rage by relating a tale of an unfaithful princess who betrayed her prince.

Danilo storms off to seek diversion at Maxim's.

Hanna rejoices after she realizes that Danilo's anger over her engagement to another man proves his love for her.

Act 3: a party at Hanna's, replicating Maxim's

Hanna has arranged a party; for Danilo's benefit, it is decorated as Maxim's.

Valencienne, dressed as a grisette, dances a can-can with the girls form Maxim's: Dodo, Lolo, Frou-Frou, Clo-Clo and Margot.

Danilo arrives, after finding the real Maxim's empty. He has just received a telegram confirming the imminent bankruptcy of Pontevedro and immediately invokes his Pontvedrian patriotism by persuading Hanna to give up her plan to marry Camille.

Hanna informs Danilo that she did not have a rendezvous with Camille in the pavilion, but rather, she was protecting the reputation of a married woman (Valencienne).

Njegus produces the fan. Zeta recognizes it as his wife Valencienne's fan and becomes infuriated; he vows to divorce Valencienne and marry Hanna himself. But Valencienne assures her husband of her fidelity by pointing to the declaration she wrote on the fan: "I am a respectable wife".

Hanna also reminds Zeta that she would lose her fortune if she remarried: under Pontevedrian law her inheritance would become the property of her new husband.

Hanna and Danilo can no longer disguise their love for one another.

Danilo becomes ecstatic as he resigns himself to his fate: he has rescued his country from bankruptcy, and he has also become the beneficiary of Hanna Glawari's wealth.

Everyone reflects anew on the enigma of understanding women as Hanna and Danilo celebrate their love by dancing to the strains of "The Merry Widow Waltz."

The Merry Widow Waltz
"Lippen schweigen, 'sflüstern Geigen: hab' mich lieb:"
("Lips are silent, whispering violins: Love me!")

Moderato
HANNA and DANILO

Lippen Schweigen, 'sflüstern Geigen: hab' mich lieb!

Libretto

Act I

Ponteverdrian Embassy in Paris.

Cascada:
Verehrteste Damen und Herren,
ich halt es für Gastespflicht,
den Hausherrn dankend zu feiern.
Doch Redner - das bin ich nicht!
Ich sag darum in aller Kürze,
die bekanntlich immer die Würze:
der Baron gab heute sein Bestes,
wir bringen ihm ein dreifach Hoch!

Cascada:
Ladies and gentlemen,
I consider it a duty of a guest
to thank the host.
But I am not a speaker!
So therefore, in all brevity,
well-known as the soul of wit:
the Baron gave his best today,
so we salute him with a triple toast!

Chor:
Dreimal Hoch der Geber des Festes!

Chorus:
A triple toast to the giver of festivities!

Zeta:
Wenn Beifall dieser Abend findet,
den man mir herzlich dargebracht,
so hat dies nicht nur mich als Hausherrn,
auch als Gesandten stolz gemacht!
Des Festes höhere Bestimmung
ist nicht nur Amusement allein;
sie gilt dem Geburtstag des Fürsten,
dem patriotisch wir uns weihn!
Bin Landesvater per procura,
drum rührt mich patriotisch dies,
denn ich bin also in figura
Pontevedro in Paris.

Zeta:
If this evening finds your approval,
as you have generously shown,
I shall not only be your host,
but also your proud ambassador!
Our lofty goal
is not for amusement alone;
but to celebrate the birthday
of our prince,
the father of our country.
Therefore, I express patriotic pride
as the representative
of Pontevedro in Paris.

**Valencienne, Sylvane, Olga,
Praskowia, Camille, St. Brioche, Zeta,
Cascada, Kromow, Chor:**
Als Landesvater per procura
da rührt ihn patriotisch dies,
denn er ist also in figura
Pontevedro in Paris!

**Valencienne, Sylvane, Olga,
Praskowia, Camille, St. Brioche, Zeta,
Cascada, Kromow, Chorus:**
He feels patriotic pride,
for he is also recognized
as the representative
of Pontevedro in Paris!

Valencienne:
So kommen Sie, s'st niemand hier!

Valencienne:
Come on, there's no one here!

Camille:
Sie sehn den glücklichsten Mann in mir!

Camille:
You see the most fortunate man in me!

Valencienne:
Ich habe mit Ihnen zu sprechen!

Valencienne:
I must talk to you!

Camille:
Ich möchte Ihnen ein Wort nur sagen!

Valencienne:
O, still! Sie wissen, dass ich dies nicht
hören will!

Camille:
Sag ich's auch nicht. Sie hören es doch!
Nur einmal möchte ich es sagen noch!

Valencienne:.
Ach, liebster Freund, warum sich so
quälen? Wir machen ein Ende!

Camille:
Ein Ende?

Valencienne:
Ich will Sie vermählen!

Camille:
Vermählen mich? Nie darf das sein!
Ich liebe nur dich, nur dich allein!

Valencienne:
Ach bitte schön, still!
Sie wissen, dass ich dies nicht hören will!
Ich bin eine anständige Frau und nehm's
mit der Ehe genau. Ich will derlei Aventüren
um gar keinen Preis mehr riskieren!
Es ist ja ein törichtes Spiel, das niemals
uns führt ans Ziel!
Sie wissen das, hoff ich, genau!
Ich bin eine anständige Frau!
Ich kann nur verlieren, und sie nichts
gewinnen, drum müssen der Lokkung
wir eiligst entrinnen.
Gib acht! Gib acht, mein Freund, gib acht!
Und spiele mit dem Feuer nicht!
Eh Du's gedacht, wirds rasch entfacht,
aus Funken eine Flamme bricht!
Sehr gefährlich ist des Feuers Macht,
wenn man sie nicht bezähmt, bewacht!
Wer das nicht kennt, sich leicht verbrennt!
Nimm vor dem Feuer dich in acht!

Camille:
I just want to say one word to you!

Valencienne:
Oh, quiet! You know that I do not want
to hear it!

Camille::
If I don't say, you'll hear it anyway!
Only this once, I want to say it again!

Valencienne:
Oh, dear friend, why torture yourself so
much? Let's put an end to this!

Camille:
An end?

Valencienne:
I want to marry you!

Camille:
Marry me? That will never happen!
I only love you, only you alone!

Valencienne:
Oh please, be still!
You know that I don't want to hear this!
I am a respectable woman and I take
marriage seriously, so I do not want to
risk any more adventures!
It's an absurd game that never leads us to
a resolution!
You know that very well, I hope!
I am a respectable woman!
I can only lose, and you gain nothing,
so we have to escape from this enticement
in a hurry.
Watch out! Watch out, my friend, be careful!
And don't play with fire!
Before you know it, it is quickly kindled,
and from sparks a flame breaks out!
The fire's power is very dangerous if one
does not tame it!
One who does not know that is easily
burned! So watch out for the fire!

Camille:
Sie sind eine anständige Frau, das weiss
ich ja leider genau.
Doch können sie wirlkich mir glauben,
Sie predigen hier einem Tauben.
Erreich' ich auch niemals mein Ziel,
erkaltet doch nie mein Gefühl.
Ich werde noch alt und noch grau sie
bleiben die anständige Frau!
Ich kenn' die Gefahren, ich muss sie
ertragen!
Ich kann Ihnen nimmer und nimmer
entsagen!

Valencienne:
Gib acht, gib acht, mein Freund, gib acht!
Und spiele mit dem Feuer nicht!
Eh! Du's gedacht, wirds rasch entfacht,
aus Funken eine Flamme bricht!
Sehr gefährlich ist des Feuers Macht,
wenn man sie nicht bezähmt, bewacht!
Wer das nicht kennt, sich leicht verbrennt!
Nimm vor dem Feuer Dich in acht!

Camille:
Ich hab's gedacht, ich hab's gedacht!
Sie pred'gen nur von Pflicht!
Das Liebesglück mir nimmer lacht, denn
liebe ist das nicht!
Wenn die Liebe spricht, gib acht, gib acht!
So ist dies nicht der Liebe Macht!
Denn wahre Liebe wagt und nimmt sich
nie in acht!

Camille:
You are a respectable woman.
Unfortunately, I know that too well.
But you must believe me, you are
preaching to deaf ears.
Even if I never reach my goal, my feelings
will never cool off,
even though I'll become old and gray,
and you remain the respectable wife!
I know the dangers I face,
and I must bear them!
I can never renounce you, and I will never
abandon you!

Valencienne:
Watch out, my friend, watch out!
And do not play with fire!
Before you know it, it will be quickly
blazing; from a spark a flame breaks out!
The fire's power is very dangerous:
if one does not tame it, watch out!
One who does not know that, he easily
burns himself! Watch out for the fire!

Camille:
I thought so, I thought so!
You preach only about duty!
The love of happiness never smiles upon
me, for that is not love!
When love speaks, watch out, watch out!
Then this is not the power of love!
Because true love always dares and never
cares!

*Zeta seeks Danilo: the fatherland needs him. Hanna Glawari, widow of the
Pontevedrian Court Banker, must not marry a Parisian.
Danilo represents the only hope of keeping her wealth in Pontevedro.*

Hanna:
Bitte, meine Herr'n! Welche Galantrie'n...

Cascada:
Sie sind der Sterne schönster Stern.
Die hier strahlend zieh'n...

Hanna:
Bitte nicht doch. 'S ist genug!
Doch jetzt geendet!

Hanna:
Please, gentlemen, such gallantries...

Cascada:
You are the most beautiful star here.
The most gleaming...

Hanna:
Please, no more. That's enough!
Now let's end it!

St. Brioche:
Und wie ein holder Sinnentrug, der uns
blendet.

Hanna:
Hören Sie! O bitte schweigen Sie!
Sie machen mich verlegen, meine Herren!

St. Brioche, Cascada, Herrenchor:
Empfangen sie die Huldigung als dieses
Festes Stern! Als schönster Stern!

Hanna:
Hab in Paris mich noch nicht ganz so
acclimatisiert, dass dieser süsse Firlefanz
von mir verstanden wird!
Bin noch Pontovedrinerin ein bischen all
zu sehr.
Ja, wär ich schon Pariserin verstünd ich
etwas mehr!
Die Herr'n sind liebenswürdig sehr gilt
das meiner Person?
Ich fürchte dies gilt mehr meiner
vielfachen Million!

St. Brioche, Cascada, Herrenchor:
O!

Hanna:
Ach, tun Sie nur nicht so!
Gar oft hab' ich's gehört, wir Witwen,
ach, wir sind begehrt!
Erst wenn wir armen Witwen reich sind,
ja, dann haben wir doppelten Wert!

Herrenchor:
Sie hat richtig gehört, Witwen die reich,
sind sehr begehrt!

St. Brioche, Cascada:
Wir sind tief gekränkt, dass man von uns
denkt, geld hätte nur Wert!

Hanna:
In unser'm Gelde liegt unser Wert,
so hab' ich's immer gehört!

St. Brioche:
She is like a lovely sensuous deceiver who
dazzles us.

Hanna:
Listen! Please, be quiet!
You embarrass me, gentlemen!

St. Brioche, Cascada, Men's Chorus:
Receive the homage as the star of this
festivity! As the most beautiful star!

Hanna:
I have not fully acclimated myself to
Paris, and I still cannot understand all
this sweet nonsense!
I am still a Pontovedrian lady, in fact, a bit
too much a lady.
Indeed, if I was already a Parisian I would
understand much more!
Aren't the men very gracious and very
kind?
I'm afraid this applies more to my wealth
than anything else!

St. Brioche, Cascada, Men's Chorus:
Oh!

Hanna:
Oh, just don't behave like that!
Often I have heard that we widows are
desired and are in great demand!
It is only when we poor widows become
rich that our value becomes double!

Men's Chorus:
You heard right, rich widows are in great
demand!

St. Brioche, Cascada:
We are deeply hurt that one thinks of us
only in terms of the value of money!

Hanna:
I have always heard that our value is only
in our money! That's how I have heard it!

St. Brioche, Cascada, Herrenchor:
Bitte nur weiter, nur weiter im Text!

St. Brioche, Cascada, Men's Chorus:
Please continue with your story!

Herrenchor:
Welch and're Wahrheit folgt zunächst?

Men's Chorus:
What other truths follows next?

Hanna:
Bei mir daheim ist's nicht der Brauch
dass Damen man hofiert, mit Komplimenten
wird man auch fast niemals molestiert!
Geht einer gar ins Zeug so scharf, so
unverschämt wie Sie, dann weiss man
wohl, dass er es darf, denn heucheln wird
er nie!

Hanna:
In my homeland it is not the custom
that ladies are courted, and they are
almost never bothered with compliments!
If anyone goes so far to be so outrageous
and insolent, then you know well that it is
acceptable, for then he could never play
the hypocrite!

St. Brioche, Cascada, Herrenchor:
Diese Weise macht sie doppelt so reizend!
Darum preise ich Sie voll Sympathie!

St. Brioche, Cascada, Men's Chorus:
This wisdom makes her doubly attractive!
That's why I prize her sympathy!

Hanna:
Lassen Sie dies fade Schmeicheln!
Ich durchschaue Euer Heucheln!
Ja! Ja! Ja!, ja!, ja...

Hanna:
Give up this insipid flattery!
I see through your hypocrisy!
Yes! Yes! Yes! Yes! Yes...

Herrenchor:
Ach nein, Gnädige, ach nein, wir können
auch ehrlich wohl sein!

Men's Chorus:
Oh no, gracious, oh no, we can also be
honest as well!

St. Brioche, Cascada:
O nicht Schmeichelei und nicht Heuchelei.
Ja, mir geht das nah!

St. Brioche, Cascada:
O no flattery and no hypocrisy.
Yes, that's hurting my feelings!

Hanna:
Ach, es geht mir gar nicht nah denn nur
Suessholz raspelt Ihr da!
Ach, ja!

Hanna:
Oh, that doesn't hurt my feelings at all,
because you are just making sweet nothings!
Oh yes!

St. Brioche:
O bitte nicht zu zweifeln da!

St. Brioche:
Please don't doubt her!

Cascada:
O bitte, ich mein's ehrlich ja!

Cascada:
Please, I honestly mean it!

St. Brioche, Cascada:
Und mir geht's wirklich sehr nah!

St. Brioche, Cascada:
And I mean it, honestly indeed!

Herrenchor:
Wir meinen's ehrlich, ach ja!

Men's Chorus:
We mean it, honestly, yes!

Zeta and is wife Valencienne welcome Hanna. Hanna invites them all to a Pontevedrian party at her villa the next day. Danilo enters, slightly tipsy.

Danilo:
O Vaterland du machst bei Tag mir schon
genügend Müh und Plag!
Die Nacht braucht jeder Diplomat doch
meistenteils für sich priate!
Um Eins bin ich schon im Büro, doch bin
ich gleich drauf anderswo, weil man den
ganzen lieben Tag nicht immer im Büro
sein mag!

Erstatte ich beim Chef Bericht so tu' ich
meistens selber nicht, die Sprechstund'
halt' ich niemals ein, ein Diplomat muss
schweigsam sein!
Die Akten häufen sich bei mir, ich finde's
gibt zu viel Papier; ich tauch die Feder selten
ein und komm doch in die Tint' hinein!
Kein Wunder wenn man so viel tut, dass
man am Abend gerne ruht, und sich bei
Nacht, was man so nennt, erholung nach
der Arbeit gönnt!

Da geh' ich zu Maxim, dort bin ich sehr
intim, ich duze alle Damen ruf' sie beim
Kosenamen, Lolo, Dodo, Jou-jou, Clo-clo,
Margot, Frou-frou, sie lassen mich
vergessen das teu're Vaterland!
Dann wird champagnisiert, und häufig
pamponiert, (cancaniert) und geht's an's
Kosen, Küssen, mit allen diesen Süssen;
Lolo, Dodo, Jou-jou, Clo-clo, Margot,
Frou-frou, dann kann ich leicht vergessen
das teu're Vaterland!

Danilo:
O Fatherland you plague me by day and
cause me sufficient toil and trouble!
Every diplomat needs the night for
privacy for themselves!
I'm already in the office, but right away
I'm ready to go somewhere else, because
no one wants to be in the office for the
entire day!

I report to the boss but honestly I usually
do not do it myself. I never keep
appointments because a diplomat must be
quiet and discreet!
The official documents pile up; I think
there is too much paper around; I seldom
dip the quill and still get the tint anyway!
No wonder if you do so much that you l
gladly rest in the evening; and treat
yourself at night to what you call
relaxation after work!

Then I go to Maxim's where I am very
intimate. I address all the ladies with
"Du" and by their pet names: Lolo, Dodo,
Jou-jou, Clo-clo, Margot, Frou-frou.
They let me forget the dear fatherland!
Then we drink champagne, and often
carouse (do the can can) and then I go on
hugging and kissing with all these cuties:
Lolo, Dodo, Jou-jou Clo-clo, Margot,
Frou-frou. Then I can easily forget my
dear fatherland!

Danilo staggers to his desk and takes a nap. When he awakens, he recognizes Hanna. Hanna mentions that since she is now in Paris she might find it interestng to marry again. (Danilo's uncle had refused to allow his nephew marry Hanna, a commoner — obvously a sore point with Hanna.)

Zeta explains Danilo's mission: that he must immedaitely marry Hanna so that her wealth remains in the coffers of the bankrupt Pontevedrian state. Danilo is skeptical, and finally states categorically that he will never marry Frau Hanna Glawari.

Valencienne:
Ein trautes Zimmerlein im Abend
Dämmerschein. Zwei Menschen ganz
allein O könnten wir es sein?

Valencienne:
A cozy little room in the evening twilight.
Two people all alone.
Could it be us?

Camille:
Ja, was? Gewiss! Wie süss!
Da sage ich nicht "nein."

Camille:
Yes, what? Certainly! How sweet!
Then I won't say "no."

Valencienne:
Wir sitzen still bei-nand' und halten Hand
in Hand ein Zauber hält uns süss gebannt!

Valencienne:
We sit quietly together holding hands as
the magic keeps us sweetly bound!

Camille:
Was dann? Ganz stumm? Warum?

Camille:
What then? Entirely silent? Why?

Valencienne, Camille:
Das ist der Zauber der stillen
Häuslichkeit.
Die Welt liegt draussen so fern, so fern
und weit!
Das ist der Zauber, der uns gefangen hält,
wir sind für uns allein die ganze Welt!

Valencienne, Camille:
This is the magic world which holds us
captive.
The world outside is so distant, yes, so
far and wide!
That is the magic that holds us captive;
we are alone in the entire world!

Valencienne:
Ja, wenn man es so recht betrachtet, wo
findet man das Lebens-glück?
Dort, wo das Leben lärmend braust?
Dort wo's in stillen friedlich haust?
Ja, wenn man es so recht betrachtet, gibt's
einen einz-gen Zufluchtsort das ist das
Haus, das ist das Heim, dort ist das
Glück, nur dort, nur dort!

Valencienne:
Yes, if you take a good look at it,
where can one find happiness in life?
Where life noisily rages?
When one is home in quiet freedom?
Yes, if you look at it, there's only a single
place for refuge.
That is the house; that is the home.
There's happiness, only there, only there!

Camille:
Was nun? Wie schad! Verzicht?
Ich sage nein und nein! Oh weh!
Ein Traum! Das kaum!

Camille:
What now? How unfortunate!
Resignation? I say, "no and no!" Oh, dear!
A dream! Hardly!

Valencienne:
Doch geht es leider nicht!
Drum leisten Sie Verzicht!
Es muss ja leider sein!
Es muss ein Ende sein!
Ein Luftschloss ist es nur!

Valencienne:
But unfortunately it is impossible!
That's why you must be resigned!
It must, unfortunately, be so!
There must be an end to it!
It is only a castle in the sky!

Von Wahrheit keine Spur!
Das ist der Zauber der stillen Häuslichkeit!
Die Welt liegt draussen so fern, so fern
und so weit!
Das ist der Zauber, der uns gefangen hält,
wir sind für uns allein die ganze Welt!
Wir wärn für uns ganz allein die ganze
Welt!

No trace of truth!
That's the magic of quiet domesticity!
The world lies so far outside, so distant
and far away!
That is the magic that holds us captive.
We are alone in the entire world!
We would be completely alone in the
entire world!

Herrenchor:
Damenwahl!
Hört man rufen rings im Saal!
Ach, Madam, nun hoffentlich kommt
doch die Reihe jetzt an mich?
O bitte, diese Tour, ach, diese einzige nur!
Ja, überglücklich wäre ich fiel doch die
Wahl auf mich!

Men's Chorus:
Ladies choice!
You hear it ringing around the hall!
Oh, madam, I hope this round of dancing
becomes mine?
Oh please, yes, I would be overjoyed if
your choice for this one would be me!

Hanna:
Meine Herr'n, im Prinzipe hätt' ich nichts
dagegen, doch die Konkurrenz so Vieler
macht mich ganz verlegen, da ich nicht
beleid'gen will, sitz die Tour ich lieber
still, 'sgibt doch Damen hier die Masse!

Hanna:
My gentlemen, in principle, I have
nothing against it, but so many of you
competing embarrasses me. I don't want
to offend anyone, so I'll sit this one out;
there are many ladies here in the crowd!

Herrenchor:
Eine Tour! Eine nur! Eine einz'ge Tour!

Men's Chorus:
A tour! Only one! A single dance!

Danilo:
Doch ist keine so bei Kasse!
Zudringlich auf mein Ehrenwort!
Diese Knaben müssen fort!
Knäblein, bettelt ruhig weiter!
Ich hole einige Blitzableiter!

Danilo:
But none is as rich as a cash register!
Intrusive on my word of honor!
These boys must be gone!
Little boys, just keep on begging!
I'll get you some lightning rods!

Cascada:
Es gibt keine gröss're Beleidigung,
Und nichts, daß so schmerzlich
verstimmt, als wenn auf dem Ball eine
Dame so gar nicht Notiz von uns nimmt!

Cascada:
There is no greater insult and nothing that
annoys one so painfully as when,
at a ball, a lady does not even take notice
of us!

St. Brioche:
Es kämpfen die Damen schon lange
um das nämliche Recht mit dem Mann,
jetzt haben Madam' hier das Wahlrecht,
und fangen damit gar nichts an!

St. Brioche:
The ladies have been fighting for a long
time for the same right as a man.
Now, Madam has the right to choose and
still makes no choice!!

Cascada:
Drum agitier' ich...

St. Brioche:
Drum affichier' ich...

Cascada, St. Brioche:
Ach, bitte lesen Sie mein Wahlplakat!

Cascada:
Wählen Sie doch Cascada...

St. Brioche:
Wählen Sie doch St. Brioche..

Cascada, St. Brioche:
Das ist der würdigste Tanzkandidat!

Cascada:
Wählen Sie doch Cascada!

Herrenchor:
Wählen Sie nicht Cascada!

St. Brioche:
Wählen Sie doch St. Brioche!

Herrenchor:
Wählen Sie nicht St. Brioche!

Cascada, St. Brioche:
Das ist der würdigste Tanzkandidat!

Herrenchor:
Ich bin der würdigste Tanzkandidat!

Hanna:
Darauf muß ich Ihnen entgegnen,
verhaßt ist mir Politik, verdirbt sie beim
Mann den Charakter, so raubt sie uns
Frauen den Schick!
Doch wollt Ihr durchaus kandidieren
und leistet auf mich nicht Verzicht,
und gibt mir das Ballrecht das Wahlrecht,
erfüll' ich die Ballbürgerpflicht!

Cascada:
That's why I'm agitated...

St. Brioche:
That's why I'm a wallflower...

Cascada, St. Brioche:
Oh, please read my campaign poster!

Cascada:
Vote for Cascada...

St. Brioche:
Vote for St. Brioche...

Cascada, St. Brioche:
That is the worthiest dance contestant!

Cascada:
Vote for Cascada!

Men's Chorus:
Don't vote for Cascada!

St. Brioche:
Vote for St. Brioche!

Men's Chorus:
Don't vote for St. Brioche!

Cascada, St. Brioche:
That is the worthiest dance contestant!

Men's Chorus:
I'm the worthiest dance contestant!

Hanna:
Then I must answer you; I find politics
hateful, if it spoils the man!
Then, it robs women of their
sophistication!
But you still want to campaign and don't
give me the right to refuse, and if the rules
of the ball give me the right to vote, I'll
fulfill my duty and follow the ball rules!

Cascada:
Dann agitier' ich!

St. Brioche:
Dann affichier'ich!

Hanna:
Ich kenn ja ganz genau Ihr Wahlplakat!
Kann es nicht verhehlen, schwer fällt mir
das Wählen, wer ist der würdigste
Tanzkandidat?

Cascada, St. Brioche, Herrenchor:
Bitte mich zu wählen!
Ich bin der würdigste Tanzkandidat!

Hanna:
Aber meine Herr'n!
Sie wollen also durchaus mit mir tanzen?
Also gut! Ich bin bereit!

Frauenchor:
Damenwahl! Damenwahl!

Danilo:
Hilfe kommt zur rechten Zeit!
O kommet doch, o kommt, Ihr
Ballsirenen,
Folgt den süssen Walzertönen!
Wie sie singen und klingen, o, tanzt doch
mit, hebt eure Füßchen ein bißchen im
Walzerschritt!
O kommet doch, o kommt, Ihr
Ballsirenen, zögert nicht das Fest zu
krönen, seht, da steht ein Tänzerheer!

Eine Dame:
Also bitte, bitte sehr!

Danilo:
Wie die Blumen im Lenze erblüh'n, und in
leuchtenden Farben erglüh'n, so erblühet
in rosigster Glut lockend der Töne Flut.
Wenn die Geige so zaubrisch erklingt
und Musik sich den Reigen erzwingt,
dann frisch auf, zögert nicht,
denn die Jugend sie spricht:

Cascada:
Then I'll become agitated!

St. Brioche:
Then I'll hang the posters!

Hanna:
I know very well your campaign poster!
I cannot conceal it, it falls heavily on me
to vote who is the most worthy dance
candidate?

Cascada, St. Brioche, Men's Chorus:
Please choose me!
I am the most worthy dance candidate!

Hanna:
But, my gentlemen!
So you really want to dance with me?
All right then! I am ready!

Women's Chorus:
Ladies' choice! Ladies' choice!

Danilo:
Help comes at the right time!
Oh come on, come on, you ball sirens,
follow the sweet tones of the waltz!
How they sing and sound!
O, dance along with them, and lift your
little feet and follow the music with the
waltz steps!
Oh come on, come on, you ball sirens.
Don't hesitate to crown the festivities.
See, there is an army of dancers waiting!

A Lady:
Now please, if you please!

Danilo:
As the flowers bloom in spring, and
glow in bright colors, the enticing flood of
tones blossom in the rosy glow. When the
violin so magically sounds and music
forces rounds of dancing, then, get up,
don't hesitate, for youth is speaking: it's
the dance, the duty of gracious feet!

Frauenchor:
Bitte sehr, wir zögern nicht!

Alles:
O kommet doch, o kommt, ihr
Ballsirenen, folgt den süssen Walzertönen.
Wie sie singen und klingen.
O, tanzt doch mit, hebt Eure Füßchen ein
bißchen im Walzerschritt!
Ja, so ist's recht und schön,
ihr Ballsirenen.
Tanzet lustig, meine Schönen,
fröhlich singt mit hellen Tönen,
so lang der Walzer klingt tanzt leicht
beschwingt!

Danilo:
O Vaterland, du machst bei Tag mir schon
genügend Müh' und Plag'.
Für Nachtdienst dank' ich, Herr Baron,
da geb' ich meine Demission!

Cascada:
Madam', darf jetzt ich hoffen?

St. Brioche:
Ich seh' den Himmel offen!

Hanna:
Ich habe nun die Qual der Wahl.

Danilo:
Der Fall ist immer noch fatal!

Hanna:
Na, schön! Wen soll ich wählen?

Valencienne:
Dürft' ich den Tänzer empfehlen?

Danilo:
Sapperment! Ein neuer Konkurrent!

Valencienne:
Der junge Mann tanzt Polka, ich hab' es
ausprobiert.

Women's Chorus:
Please, we do not hesitate!

Everyone:
Oh come on, o come, you ball-lovers,
follow the sweet waltz melodies, as they
sing and sound.
O, dance along with them, lift your little
feet a bit to the steps of the waltz steps!
Yes, that's right and lovely,
you ball-lovers.
Dance cheerfully, my beautiful ones,
and merrily sings its bright melodies,
if the waltz sounds, dance to its lively
beat!

Danilo:
O Fatherland, you make enough trouble
and trials for me by day.
Thanks for the night duty, Baron, I will
resign!

Cascada: *(to Hanna)*
Madam, may I hope now?

St. Brioche:
I see heaven opening!

Hanna:
I'm now having the torture of choosing.

Danilo: *(to himself)*
The case is still fatal!

Hanna:
Well, fine! Who should I choose?

Valencienne: *(with Camille arriving)*
May I recommend a dance partner?

Danilo:
By Jove! A new competitor!

Valencienne:
The young man is dancing the polka,
I've tried it out.

Auch tanzt famos er Mazurka,
ich hab' es ausprobiert.
Nach rechts und links kann er tanzen,
ich hab' es ausprobiert.
Im Walzer hat er excelliert, drum wird er
von mir protegiert!
Drum agitier' ich und affichier' ich,
ach bitte, hören Sie mein Wahlplakat!
Wählen Sie doch Rosillon!
Er ist der würdigste Tanzkandidat!

Cascada:
Wählen Sie nur Cascada!

Herrenchor:
Wählen Sie nicht Rosillon!

St. Brioche:
Wählen Sie nur St. Brioche!

Herrenchor:
Wählen Sie nicht Rosillon!

Hanna:
Aha, schon wieder ein Tanzkandidat!
candidate!

Valencienne, Cascada, St. Brioche:
Er ist der würdigste Tanzkandidat!

Herrenchor:
Ich bin der würdigste Tanzkandidat!

Camille:
Pardon, Madam', zu viel Reklam!

Hanna:
Das find' ich nicht, doch nein...
den ich als Tänzer möchte, ist Einer, der
sich gibt den Schein, als ob ich ihm egal
möcht' sein.

Sie sind wohl der Rechte!

Danilo:
Ich? Gnädige Frau, ich tanze nicht!

He also dances the mazurka,
I've also tried it.
He can dance to the right and left,
I've tried it.
In the waltz he excelled, that's why he is
sponsoring me!
That's why I'm agitating and affix posters,
oh please, listen to my campaign!
Do vote for Rosillon!
He is the worthiest dance candidate!

Cascada:
Just vote for Cascada!

Men's Chorus:
Don't vote for Rosillon!

St. Brioche:
Just vote for St. Brioche!

Men's Chorus:
Don't vote for Rosillon!

Hanna:
Aha, once again, another dance
candidate!

Valencienne, Cascada, St. Brioche:
He is the worthiest dance candidate!

Men's Chorus:
I'm the worthiest dance candidate!

Camille:
Pardon, madam, too much advertising!

Hanna:
I do not think so, but no, that...
I want as a dancer, *(to herself),* one who
gives himself the appearance, as if I don't
make a difference to him.
(to Danilo)
You are probably the right one!

Danilo:
Me? Gracious lady, I do not dance!

Hanna:
So leisten Sie kurzweg Verzicht?

Danilo:
Verzicht? O, nein!
Der Tanz ist doch wohl mein?

Hanna:
Gewiss! Warum?

Danilo:
Nun, da der Tanz mein Eigentum, so darf
mit ihm ich alles tun, was mir beliebt,
nicht wahr?

Hanna:
Nun, ja?

Valencienne, Camille, St. Brioche:
Was treibt er da?

Danilo:
Der Tanz, den mir die Gnädige gewährt,
ist doch wohl zehntausend Francs wohl wert!
Mir gehört der Tanz, ich verlang' dafür
Zehntausend Francs zu wohltätigem Zweck!

Camille, St. Brioche, Cascada, Herrenchor:
'S ist unerhört!

Danilo:
Für diesen Preis geb' ich ihn weg!

St. Brioche, Camille, Herrenchor:
Zehntausend Francs?

St. Brioche:
Er ist verrückt!

Danilo:
Sie geh'n!
Jetzt ist es mir geglückt!

Sehen Sie, meine Gnäd'ge, sehen Sie...

Hanna:
So you abruptly renounce the claim?

Danilo:
Renounce? Oh no!
The dance is still mine, isn't it?

Hanna:
Certainly! Why?

Danilo:
Well, since the dance belongs to me,
I may do anything I want with it, that
pleases me, right?

Hanna:
Well, yes?

Valencienne, Camille, St. Brioche:
What is he pursuing over there?

Danilo:
The dance that the gracious lady granted
me is surely worth ten thousand francs!
The dance belongs to me, so I demand
ten thousand francs for a charitable cause!

Camille, St. Brioche, Cascada, Men's Chorus:
That's unheard of!

Danilo:
I'll give it away for that price!

St. Brioche, Camille, Men's Chorus:
Ten thousand francs?

St. Brioche:
He's crazy!

Danilo:
You go!
Now I am in luck!
(to Hanna)
Look, my gracious lady, you see...

Herrenchor:
Zehntausend Francs! Das ist zum lachen.

Men's Chorus:
Ten thousand francs! That's laughable.

Cascada:
Zehntausend Francs!

Cascada:
Ten thousand francs!

St. Brioche:
Das ist zum lachen!

St. Brioche:
That's laughable!

Danilo:
Wie sie aus dem Staub sich machen.
Zahlen wollen die Herren nie!
Ein Griff ins Portmonnaie tut ihnen
furchtbar weh.
So sind die Herren heutzutag, ein wirklich
nobler Schlag!

Danilo:
How they leave us in the dust.
The gentlemen never want to pay up!
One grab of their wallets hurts them
terribly.
Such are the gentlemen of today:
a real noble type!

Camille:
Den Angriff muss ich gleich parieren.
Die zehntausend Francs, die gebe ich!

Camille: *(to Valencienne)*
I have to ward off the attack right now.
I'll give the ten thousand francs!

Valencienne:
Sind Sie schon verliebt?

Valencienne:
Are you already in love?

Camille:
Sie wünschten doch selbst...

Camille: *(astonished)*
But, you yourself....

Valencienne:
Untersteh'n Sie sich!

Valencienne:
Don't you dare!

Danilo:
Der Letzte ging. Sie sind befreit, und jetzt,
gnädige Frau, bin ich zum Tanz bereit!

Danilo:
The last one left. You are liberated, and
now, Madam, I am ready for the dance!

Hanna:
Jetzt danke ich sehr!

Hanna:
Now I'll thank you very much!

Danilo:
Und mein Mandat! Sie wählten mich doch?

Danilo:
And my mandate! You voted for me?

Hanna:
O, Sie Hauptdiplomat! Ich tanze nicht!

Hanna:
Oh, you arch-diplomat! I will not dance!

Danilo:
Geigen erklingen, locken so süss,
werden Sie zwingen, gewiss!

Danilo:
Violins are sounding, so sweetly enticing.
They will surely force you!

Hanna:
Nein, ich will nicht!

Hanna:
No, I do not want to!

Danilo:
Aber, gnädige Frau, kommen Sie!

Danilo:
But, madam, come!

Hanna:
Sie abscheulicher mann!

Hanna:
You abominable man!

After resisting Danilo, Hanna suddenly flies into his arms and dances with him.

Wie prächtig Sie tanzen!

How splendidly you dance!

Danilo:
Ach, man tut was man kann!

Danilo:
Oh, one does what one can!

End of Act I

Act II

The next day. A garden party at Hanna's villa in Paris.
Guests celebrate the birthday of the Grand Duke of Pontevedro.

Hanna:
Ich bitte hier jetzt zu verweilen,
wo allsogleich nach heimatlichem Brauch,
das fest des Fürsten so begangen wird,
als ob man in Letijne wär daheim.

Hanna:
I beg you to remain. Right now,
according to the custom of our homeland,
we celebrate a feast to honor the Prince,
as if we were home in Letijne.

Chor:
Mi velimo dase dase Veslimo!
Mi velimo dase dase Veslimo!
Lasst uns jauchzen und lasst uns singen!
Lasst uns tanzen und lasst uns springen!
Lasst uns jauchzen und lasst uns singen!
Lasst uns tanzen und lasst uns springen!
Mi velimo dase dase Veslimo! Hei!

Chorus:
Mi velimo das das das Veslimo!
Mi velimo dase dases Veslimo!
Let us rejoice and let us sing!
Let us dance and let us jump!
Let us rejoice and let us sing!
Let us dance and let us spring!
Mi velimo dase dases Veslimo! Hei!

Hanna:
Nun lasst uns aber wie daheim jetzt
singen unser'n Ringelreim von einer Fee,
die wie bekannt daheim die Vilja wird
genannt!
Es lebt' eine Vilja, ein Waldmägdelein,
ein Jäger erschaut' sie im Felsengestein!
Dem Burschen, dem wurde so eigen zu
Sinn, er schaute und schaut' auf das
Waldmägdlein hin.

Hanna:
Well, let's do as we do at home,
and sing our ringing tune
about a fairy who is known at home
as Vilja!
There lived a Vilja, a wood-maiden,
who a hunter spied on a rocky cliff!
The boy became so affected that he
kept staring and staring at the little
wood-maiden.

Und ein niegekannter Schauder fasst den
jungen Jägersmann, sehnsuchtsvoll fing er
still zu seufzen an!

And a sudden shudder seized the young
hunter, who longingly began to sigh
silently!

Vilja, o Vilja, du Waldmägdelein,
fass' mich und lass' mich dein
Trautliebster sein!
Vilja, O Vilja, was tust Du mir an?
Bang fleht ein liebkranker Mann!

Vilja, o Vilja, you little wood-maiden,
take me and let me be your true love
forever!
Vilja, O Vilja, what are you doing to me?
A lovesick man fearfully begs for you!

Chor:
Vilja, o Vilja, Du Waldmägdelein,
fass' mich und lass' mich dein
Trautliebster sein!

Chorus:
Vilja, o Vilja, you little wood-maiden,
take me and let me be your true love
forever!

Hanna:
Vilja, O Vilja, was tust Du mir an?
Bang fleht ein liebkranker Mann!
Das Waldmägd'lein streckte die Hand
nach ihm aus und zog ihn hinein in ihr
felsiges Haus.

Dem Burschen die Sinne vergangen fast
sind, so liebt und so küsst gar kein
irdisches Kind.

Als sie sich dann satt geküsst
verschwand sie zu derselben Frist!
Einmal hat noch der Arme sie gegrüsst:
Vilja, o Vilja, Du Waldmägdelein,
fass' mich und lass' mich
dein Trautliebster sein!
Vilja, O Vilja, was tust Du mir an?
Bang fleht ein liebkranker Mann!

Chor:
Vilja, o Vilja, Du Waldmägdelein,
fass' mich und lass' mich dein
Trautliebster sein!

Hanna:
Vilja, O Vilja, was tust Du mir an?
Bang fleht ein liebkranker Mann!

Chor:
Mi velimo dase dase Veslimo!
Mi velimo dase dase Veslimo!
Lasst uns jauchzen und lasst uns singen!
Lasst uns tanzen und lasst uns springen!
Lasst uns jauchzen und lasst uns singen!
Lasst uns tanzen und lasst uns springen!
Mi velimo dase dase Veslimo! Hei!

Hanna:
Vilja, O Vilja, what are you doing to me?
A lovesick man fearfully begs for you!
The wood-maiden stretched out her hand
to him and pulled him into her cliff
dwelling.

The boy almost lost his senses, because
no earthly person was ever loved or
kissed with such passion before.

As soon as she had enough kissing,
she immediately disappeared!
One day the poor lad greeted her:
Vilja, o Vilja, you wood-maiden,
take me and let me be your true love
forever!
Vilja, O Vilja, what are you doing to me?
A lovesick man fearfully begs for you!

Chorus:
Vilja, o Vilja, you wood-maiden,
take me and let me be your true love
forever!

Hanna:
Vilja, O Vilja, what are you doing to me?
A lovesick man fearfully begs for you!

Chorus:
Mi velimo das das das Veslimo!
Mi velimo dase dases Veslimo!
Let us rejoice and let us sing!
Let us dance and let us jump!
Let us rejoice and let us sing!
Let us dance and let us spring!
Mi velimo dase dases Veslimo! Hei!

Danilo appears. Zeta informs him that Rosillon is planning to marry Hanna.

*Hanna arrives. Alone with Danilo, she inquires why he is always avoiding her;
he counters with a tale about the "military strategy of a cavalryman."*

Hanna:
Heia, Mädel, aufgeschaut, guck' die
schmucken Reiter!
Nimmt dich einer wohl zur Braut oder
sprengt er weiter?
Heia, Mädel, lass' ihn nicht, kann als
Mann dir taugen!
Guck' ihm keck ins Gesicht, blitz' mit
deinen Augen!

Danilo:
Mädel schaut und Mädel guckt, dass es
ihm im Herzen zuckt.

Hanna:
Mädel zeigt trotzdem sie schweigt,
dass sie sich in Lieb ihm neigt.
Dummer, dummer Reitersmann
der mich nicnt verstehen kann!
Dummer, dummer Reiter, reitet, reitet weiter!
Dummer, dummer Reitersmann!
Hoplahop und hoplaho!

Dummer, dummer Reiter, reitet, reitet weiter!
Dummer, dummer Reitersmann!
Heia, Reiter, kehrt zurück, hopp, sein
Pferdchen tänzelt, wie er jetzt mit seinem
Blick bittet und scherwenzelt!
Mädel kümmert sich nicht drum, hüpft
und summt ein Tänzchen,
Reiter, du warst gar zu dumm doch ich bin
kein Gänschen!

Danilo:
Reiter guckt und Reiter lacht, willst du
nicht, nun dann gut'Nacht.
Mädel Mädel meiner Wahl, ich komm
nicht ein zweites Mal.

Hanna:
Dummer, dummer Reiter, reitet, reitet
weiter! Dummer, dummer Reitersmann!

Danilo:
Kluger, kluger Reiter, reitet, reitet Weiter!
Kluger, kluger Reitersmann!

Hanna:
Heigh ho, maiden, have a look at those
pretty riders!
Will one of them take you for his bride
or does he keep riding on?
Heigh ho, maiden, don't let him go loose;
he can serve you well as a husband!
Boldly look in his face,
and flash your eyes!

Danilo:
Maiden looks and maiden peers, till his
heart quivers.

Hanna:
Despite her silence the maiden shows that
she is not averse to loving him.
Silly, silly horseman
who cannot understand me!
Silly, silly horseman, ride, ride on!
Silly, silly horseman!
Hoplahop and hoplaho!

Silly, silly horseman, ride, ride on!
Silly, silly horseman!
Heia, horseman returns, hopp, his horse
prances, how he now pleads with her
with his tears and his gaze !
Maiden pays no attention to him,
as she hops and hums a little dance,
rider, you were all too stupid
but I am no goose!

Danilo:
Horseman looks and horseman laughs,
if you don't want to, then goodnight.
Maiden of my choice, I will not come
back a second time.

Hanna:
Silly, silly horseman, ride, ride on!
Silly, silly horseman!

Danilo:
Clever, clever horseman, ride, ride on!
Clever, clever horseman!

Hanna:
Hoplahop und hoplaho!
Dummer, dummer Reiter, reitet, reitet
weiter! Dummer, dummer Reitersmann!

Danilo:
Kluger, kluger Reiter, reitet, reitet Weiter!
Kluger, kluger Reitersmann!

Hanna:
Dummer, dummer Reiter, reitet, reitet
weiter! Dummer, dummer Reitersmann!

Hanna:
Hoplahop and hoplaho!
Silly, silly rider, ride on!
Silly, silly rider!

Danilo:
Clever, clever rider, ride, ride on!
Clever, clever rider!

Hanna:
Silly, silly rider, ride on!
Silly, silly rider!

Hanna teases Danilo, and then departs.
St. Brioche threatens Cascada with a duel if he continues to ogle Hanna.
With Zeta's interference, a fight for Hanna between Danilo and Cascada is avoided.

St. Brioche, Cascada, Chor:
Wie die Weiber...?

Danilo:
...Man behandelt?

St. Brioche, Cascada, Chor:
Hört ihn an!

Danilo:
Eine so, die And're anders,
Da gibt's keinen Feldzugsplan!

Zeta:
Dass die Weiber...

Danilo, St. Brioche, Cascada, Chor:
Dass die Weiber?

Zeta:
Treu uns bleiben...

Danilo, St. Brioche, Cascada, Chor:
Also, wie?

Zeta, Danilo:
Das hat man noch nicht ergründet,

St. Brioche, Cascada, Chor:
Da gibt's keine Theorie!

St. Brioche, Cascada, Chorus:
How these women ...?

Danilo:
... one should handle?

St. Brioche, Cascada, Chorus:
Listen to him!

Danilo:
One like this, the other that way,
there's no battle plan!

Zeta:
That women...

Danilo, St. Brioche, Cascada, Chorus:
That the women?

Zeta:
Remain faithful to us...

Danilo, St. Brioche, Cascada, Chorus:
Well, then, how?

Zeta, Danilo:
Not yet discovered,

St. Brioche, Cascada, Chorus:
For that, there's no theory yet!

Danilo:
Der Einen macht man Complimente
so und so, und do und so!

Zeta:
Und schmeichelt, streichelt ohne Ende:
so und so, und do und so!

St. Brioche:
Der Andern, muß man imponieren:
so und so, und do und so!

Cascada:
Man darf sie auch sogar sekieren:
so und so, und do und so!

Danilo:
Die Schwipse, die nach Haus' wir bringen:
so und so, und do und so!
Die Dritte, die will Zärtlichkeiten:
so und so, und so und so!
Doch auswärts sind wir lose Falter:
so und so, und do und so!

Zeta:
Haus markieren will das Alter:
so und so, und do und so!
Die Vierte die will zanken, streiten:
so und so, und do und so!

Cascada:
Die Fünfte will nur tanzen, lachen:
So und so, und do und so!

Danilo, Zeta, St. Brioche, Cascada:
Dann wollen sie auch and're Sachen!
so und so, und do und so!

Danilo, Zeta:
Ja, das Studium der Weiber is schwer
nimmt uns männer verteufelt auch her!
Niemals kennt doch an Seele und Leib
Man das Weib.

Chor:
Ach, die Weiber, diese Weiber!
Weib, Weib, Weib, Weib!

Danilo:
The one you give compliments, so and so,
and do and so!

Zeta:
And flatters, caresses without end:
so and so, and do and so!

St. Brioche:
For the others, one must be strong:
so and so, and do and so!

Cascada:
One may even tease them:
so and so, and do and so!

Danilo:
The swiping that we bring home:
so and so, and do and so!
The third one, wants tender caresses:
so and so, and do and so!
But outwardly, we are loose butterflies:
so and so, and do and so!

Zeta:
The old one wants to age in the house:
so and so, and do and so!
The fourth wants to quarrel and argue:
so and so, and do and so!

Cascada:
The fifth only wants to dance and laugh:
so and so, and do and so!

Danilo, Zeta, St. Brioche, Cascada:
Then they also want other things, too!
so and so, and do and so!

Danilo, Zeta:
Yes, the study of women is difficult,
and becomes a devilish task for us men!
One can never know the body and soul of
a woman.

Chorus:
Oh, the women, these women!
Wife, wife, wife, wife!

Danilo, Zeta:
Mädchen zart, Gretchenart, blondes Haar,
mit dem treuesten Blauäugleinpaar,
ob sie schwarz oder rot oder blond sind
gefärbt, 's ist egal, man wird doch gegärbt.

Chor:
Weiber, Weiber, Weiber, Weiber, ja!
Weiber, Weiber, Weiber, Weiber, ach!

Danilo, Zeta, St. Brioche, Cascada,
Chor:
Ja, das Studium der Weiber ist schwer,
nimmt uns männer verteufelt auch her!
Niemals kennt doch an Seele und Leib
Man das Weib, Weib, Weib, Weib, Weib!
Mädchen zart, Gretchenart, blondes Haar,
Mit dem treuesten Blauäugleinpaar,
Ob sie schwarz oder rot oder blond sind
gefärbt, 's ist egal, man wird doch gegärbt.

Chor:
Weiber, Weiber, Weiber, Weiber, Weiber!
Weiber, Weiber, Weiber, Weiber, Weiber!
Weiber, Weiber, Weiber, Weiber, Weiber!
Weib, Weib, Weib, Weib!

Danilo, Zeta:
Tender maiden, innocent air, blond hair,
and a most faithful pair of little blue-eyes,
whether the hair is dyed black or red or
blond, no matter, one will be smitten anyway.

Chorus:
Women, women, women, women, yes!
Women, women, women, women, ah!

Danilo, Zeta, St. Brioche, Cascada,
Chorus:
Yes, the study of women is difficult,
and becomes a devilish task for us men!
Never, after all, can one know a woman's
body and soul, wife, wife, wife, wife!
Tender maiden, innocent air, blond hair,
and a most faithful pair of little blue-eyes,
whether the hair is dyed black or red or
blond, no matter, one will be smitten anyway.

Chorus:
Women, women, women, women, women!
Women, women, women, women, women!
Women, women, women, women, women!
Wife, wife, wife, wife!

Danilo and Hanna engage in some serous flirting with one another.
They dance off and hum to the music heard from the other room.
Camille and Valencienne enter. Valencienne gives him a fan upon which she writes
a dedication: "I am a respectable wife." He tries to kiss her, but fails.

Valencienne:
Mein Freund, Vernunft!

Camille:
Wie Sie mich quälen!

Valencienne:
Ich will's. Sie müssen sich vermählen!
Sie müssen heute noch mit Hanna sprechen.

Camille:
Nun gut! Ich tu's, doch wird das Herz mir
brechen!

Valencienne:
My friend, be sensible!

Camille:
How you torture me!

Valencienne:
I insist! You must get married!
You have to speak to Hanna today.

Camille:
Very well, I'll do it, although my heart
will break!

Valencienne:
O, glauben Sie es fällt mir schwer,
auf Ihre Liebe zu verzichten,
doch muss ich mich, so will's die Ehr',
streng nach der guten Sitte richten!

Camille:
Muss ich für immer dich verlieren?

Valencienne:
Sie woll'n mich doch nicht compromettieren?

Camille:
Das will ich nicht! Das darf ich nicht!

Valencienne:
So ist es recht. So hab' ich Dich lieb.

Camille:
Ich muß dich küssen!

Valencienne:
Sie machen mich böse!

Camille:
Vergib! Vergib, mein Lieb!
Wie eine Rosenknospe im Maienlicht
erblüht, so ist in meinem Herzen
die Liebe aufgeglüht.
Das war ein selig Keimen, von dem ich
nichts geahnt, ein wundersames Träumen,
das mich ans Glück gemahnt.
Und nun das Glück gekommen, soll's
wieder, wieder fort?
Das Maienlicht verglommen?
Die Knospe sie verdorrt?
Ein jauchzend, jubelnd Singen in meiner
Seele schallt:
es wird Dich mir erringen der Liebe
Allgewalt.

Valencienne:
O Camille!

Camille:
Valencienne!

Valencienne:
Oh, believe me, it is difficult for me
to renounce your love.
But I must, since honor demands that I
follow propriety strictly!

Camille:
Must I lose you forever?

Valencienne:
You surely do not want to compromise me?

Camille:
I do not want that! I must not do that!

Valencienne:
That's right. That's the way I love you.

Camille:
I must kiss you!

Valencienne:
You're making me angry!

Camille:
Forgive! Forgive me, my love!
Like a rosebud blossoms in the light of
May, so in my heart, love has begun to
blaze.
That was a blessed sprouting, of which I
knew nothing, a wondrous dream
that foretold of happiness.
And now that happiness has come,
must it again flee?
The light of May has faded?
Did the bud wither?
A jubilant, joyful singing echoes in my
soul:
you shall be won for me, by the almighty
power of love.

Valencienne:
Oh Camille!

Camille:
Valencienne!

Valencienne:
Nein sachte, sacht!
Du hast mich um den Verstand gebracht!

Valencienne:
No, gently, gently!
You have driven me out of my mind!

Camille:
Zum Abschied, Du Süsse, einen letzten Kuss!

Camille:
Farewell, sweetheart, one last kiss!

Valencienne:
Doch nicht hier!

Valencienne:
But not here!

Camille:
Sieh dort den kleinen Pavillon, er kann
höchst diskret verschwiegen sein!
O, dieser kleiner Pavillon plaudert nicht
ein Wörtchen aus, o nein!
Dunkel uns umfängt nimm, was Liebe uns
schenkt!
Komm in den kleinen Pavillon,
komm zum süssen Rendezvous, o Du!

Camille:
See the little pavilion there, it can be
discreet and secluded!
Oh, this little pavilion does not tattle a
single word, oh no!
It embraces us in the darkness, so let's
take what love bestows upon us!
Come into the little pavilion,
come to the sweet rendezvous, o you!

Valencienne:
Ich seh' schon, ich werd' hineingeh'n müssen.

Valencienne:
I see already that I'll have to go inside.

Camille:
Komm in den kleinen Pavillon.
Lass' zum letzten Mal dich küssen, ach!

Camille:
Come into the little pavilion.
Let me kiss you for the last time, ah!

Valencienne:
Ist er verschwiegen?
Mir wird ganz schwach!

Valencienne:
Is it discreet?
I'm getting very weak!

Camille, Valencienne:
Dunkel uns umfängt nimm, was Liebe uns
schenkt!
Dort in dem dunkeln Pavillon strahlt uns
hell der süssen Liebe Lohn!

Camille, Valencienne:
It embraces us in the darkness, so let's
take what love bestows upon us!
There in the dark pavilion sweet love's
reward brightly shines for us!

*Zeta appears and inquires why the pavillon remains dark; Njegus stammers as he
informs Zeta that someone is inside the pavilion: that it is Camille Rosillon with a
lady. Zeta orders Njegus to lock the back door of the pavilion.
Danilo enters. Zeta informs him that he will peep through the pavilion keyhole to see
who is there. He becomes incensed after he recognizes his wife.
Danilo tries to calm him down. But Zeta insists on opening the pavilion door.
In the meantime, Njegus switched Hanna for Valencienne.
As Zeta yells "open up, open up," Hanna and Camille exit the pavilion together.*

Danilo:
Ha! Ha!

Zeta:
Ha! Ha!

Hanna:
Wir fragen was man von uns will?

Danilo:
Ha! Hanna und Camille!

Zeta:
War ich denn blind? Ich sah genau...

Danilo:
Ha! Hanna und Camille!
Mein ganzer Geist steht still.
Jetzt wird die Sache etwas flau!

Zeta:
Wo ist denn meine Frau?

Valencienne:
Du wünschest?

Zeta:
Ich bin dumm und starr!

Valencienne:
Was ist gescheh'n? So sprich doch klar!

Danilo:
Ha! Hanna und Camille!

Camille:
So sei doch endlich still!

Zeta:
Ich sah dort eine Dame kurz zuvor...
Ich guckte schnell durch's Schlüsselloch...

Hanna:
Das war gerade nicht sehr fein!

Danilo:
Ha! Ha!

Zeta:
Ha! Ha!

Hanna:
What do you want from us?

Danilo:
Ha! Hanna and Camille!

Zeta:
Was I blind? I saw exactly...

Danilo:
Ha! Hanna and Camille!
My whole spirit stops.
Now things are going awry!

Zeta:
Where is my wife?

Valencienne:
What did you want?

Zeta:
I'm just stupid!

Valencienne:
What happened? So speak up clearly!

Danilo:
Ha! Hanna and Camille!

Camille: *(to Danilo)*
Be quiet for once!

Zeta:
I saw a lady there just before...
I looked quickly through the keyhole...

Hanna:
That was not very nice !

Zeta:
Ich hört' und traute meine Ohren nicht...

Danilo:
Aber praktisch doch!

Zeta:
Wie dieser Herr da, ihr Liebe schwor!

Hanna:
Die Dame, die war ich!

Danilo:
Ha! Hanna!

Zeta:
Ich hätt' geschworen, es wär' meine Frau!

Hanna:
Mein lieber Camille, gesteh'n Sie's nur ein!

Valencienne:
O, dies zu hören ist Rettung und Pein!

Camille:
Ach, dies zu sagen ist!

Danilo:
Mich packt der Eifersucht fast könnte ich
schrein!

Zeta:
Ich kann's nicht glauben, o nein, o nein!

Njegus:
Das arrangierte ich ganz schlau und ganz
fein!

Hanna:
Und war der Baron so indiskret,
zu lauschen und spähen beim
Schlüsselloch,
so sagen Sie hier, was drinnen Sie mir
gestanden, ich, bitte, so sagen Sie's doch!

Zeta:
I heard but didn't trust my ears...

Danilo:
But be practical!

Zeta:
I couldn't believe it, he vowed his love!

Hanna:
That lady was me!

Danilo:
Ha! Hanna!

Zeta:
I would have sworn it was my wife!

Hanna:
My dear Camille, just admit it!

Valencienne:
To hear this is salvation and pain!

Camille:
Ah, to admit this!

Danilo:
I'm torn by jealousy, and I could almost
scream!

Zeta:
I cannot believe it, oh no!

Njegus:
I arranged that quite cleverly and quite
neatly!

Hanna:
And if the baron was so indiscreet,
as to listen and peep through the keyhole,
then tell us
what you confessed to me inside.
Please, just tell them!

Camille:
Ich soll es sagen?

Camille:
I should confess?

Danilo:
Und ich soll's ertragen?

Danilo:
And I must bear it?

Camille:
Nun, Excellenz, da ich nicht anders kann,
was ich drin sagte, so hören Sie an:

Camille:
Well, Excellency, since I can't help it,
what I said inside, sounds like this:

Zeta:
Jetzt bin ich doch neugierig, was er mir
sagen wird.

Zeta:
Now I'm really curious what he's going to
tell me.

Camille:
Wie eine Rosenknospe im Maienlicht
erblüht, so ist in meinem Herzen
die Liebe aufgeglüht.
Das war ein selig Keimen, von dem ich
nichts geahnt, ein wundersames Träumen,
das mich ans Glück gemahnt.
Und nun das Glück gekommen, soll's
wieder, wieder fort?
Das Maienlicht verglommen?
Die Knospe sie verdorrt?
Ein jauchzend, jubelnd Singen in meiner
Seele schallt:
es wird Dich mir erringen der Liebe
Allgewalt.

Camille:
Like a rosebud blossoms in the light of
May, so in my heart, love has begun to
blaze.
That was a blessed sprouting, of which I
knew nothing, a wondrous dream
that foretold of happiness.
And now that happiness has come,
must it again flee?
The light of May has faded?
Did the bud wither?
A jubilant, joyful singing echoes in my
soul:
you shall be won for me, by the almighty
power of love.

Hanna:
Er glaubt ihm wirklich Wort für Wort!
Und sein Verdacht, er ist schon fort!
Ah, lieber Graf und du bleibst ganz kalt?
Was wetten wir, du redest bald!
Redest bald!

Hanna:
He really believes him word for word!
And his suspicions are already gone!
Ah, dear Count you remain quite cold?
What shall we wager, that you speak soon!
Speak soon!

Valencienne:
Ich fasse nicht ein einzig' Wort!
Ja, will er wirklich von mir fort?
Sein Liebeslied ist kaum noch verhallt.
Er singt's vor ihr, wo mir allein
dass Lied doch galt?
Ist sie dahin so rasch, der Liebe Allgewalt!

Valencienne:
I cannot grasp a single word!
Yes, does he really want to leave me?
His love song has barely stopped.
He sings it for her, when
the song was meant for me alone!
Is love's almighty power spent so quickly!

Danilo:
Ich höre wie verschwommen, fasse auch
nicht ein Wort!
Sie hat sich schön benommen!
Mir ist's nicht vergönnt, sie zu erringen,
doch mich lässt's nicht kalt!
Will mich zur Ruhe zwingen, ich gehe und
das bald, Ja, sehr bald!

Zeta:
Der Wahn is mir nun ganz benommen,
zu ihr ist er gewiss gekommen.
Ich glaub' ihm Wort für Wort,
's war meine Frau nicht dort!
Wenn's meine Frau so triebe,
macht' ich ein Ende bald!
Bei solchen Dinge bleib' ein and'rer kalt!
Bleib' er kalt!

Hanna:
Den Herrschaften hab' ich 'was zu
erzählen!

Chor:
Nun was?

Hanna:
Dass als Verlobte sich empfehlen
Herr Rosillon...

Camille:
Was? Ich?

Valencienne:
O, Gott!

Danilo:
Ah schön!

Zeta:
Wie? Was?

Chor:
Ah, welche Neuigkeit!

Valencienne:
Bin starr!

Danilo:
I hear something blurry, and I cannot
understand a single word!
She has behaved beautifully!
I'm not destined to win her,
but I'm not indifferent to the truth!
I'll act calmly to the power and leave,
yes, I'll leave very soon!

Zeta:
My delusion has now totally faded;
he definitely went inside for Hanna.
I believe him word for word,
that it wasn't my wife in there!
If my wife had behaved like that,
I would put an end to it very soon!
Other men may take such things in stride!
Let him remain cold!

Hanna: *(relates what really happened)*
Ladies and gentlemen, I have something to
tell you!

Chorus:
Well what?

Hanna: *(glancing at Danilo)*
Mr. Rosillon has pledged himself to be
my betrothed...

Camille:
What? Me?

Valencienne:
Oh, God!

Danilo:
Ah, how nice!

Zeta:
How? What?

Chorus:
Ah, what news!

Valencienne:
I'm startled!

Camille:
Bin starr!

Danilo:
Bin starr!

Zeta:
Bin starr!

Hanna:
Die Wirkung ist ganz wunderbar!

Chor:
Wir gratulieren!

Danilo:
O, ihr verfluchten Millionen!

Zeta:
O, ihr verlor'nen Millionen!

Camille:
Das geht doch nicht!
Da muss ich protestier'n.

Hanna:
Dann werden Sie die Baronin blamier'n?

Zeta:
Sie wollen wirklich?

Valencienne:
Wirklich wollen Sie?

Hanna:
Warum denn nicht?

Zeta:
Ich bin dagegen und der Graf!

Hanna:
Sie auch?

Danilo:
O nein, warum soll ich dagegen sein?
Ich gebe Ihnen meinen Segen!
Ich meine nur...

Camille:
I'm startled!

Danilo:
I'm startled!

Zeta:
I'm startled!

Hanna: *(to herself)*
The effect is quite wonderful!

Chorus:
Congratulations!

Danilo:
Oh, you cursed millions!

Zeta:
O, you lost millions!

Camille: *(whispering)*
You can't do this!
I must protest.

Hanna: *(whispering to Camille)*
Then you'll disgrace the Baroness?

Zeta:
Do you really want to?

Valencienne: *(to Camille)*
You really want to?

Hanna:
Why not?

Zeta:
I am against it, and the count!

Hanna: *(to Danilo)*
You too?

Danilo:
Oh no, why should I be against it?
I give you my blessing!
I mean...

Hanna:
Was meinen Sie?

Danilo:
Verlieb' dich oft, verlob' dich selten,
heirate nie!
Die Ehe ist für mich privat, ich rede nur
als Diplomat, wahrhaftig nur ein
Standpunkt, der längst überwunden.
Ein Zweibund sollte stets sie sein,
doch bald stellt sich ein Dreibund ein,
der zählt oft, der zählt oft blos nach
schwachen Stunden!
Vom europäischen Gleichgewicht,
wenn einer sich verehelicht, von dem ist
bald nichts mehr zu spüren.
Der Grund liegt meistens nur darin:
es gibt Madam zu sehr sich hin der Politik
der off'nen Türen!

Hanna:
Das ist doch unverschämt!

Danilo:
Jawohl, ich schild're nicht zu stark,
s' ist etwas faul im Staate Dänemark!

Hanna:
Ein flotter Ehestand soll's sein:
ganz nach Pariser Art!
Er sagt: "Madam;" ich sag': "Monsieur,"
ganz nach Pariser Art!
Wir lieben uns, wie sich's versteht:
ganz nach Pariser Art!
Wo jeder seine Wege geht:
ganz nach Pariser Art!
Das hat Rrrasss" so, tra-la-la-la-la-la
macht mir Spasss' so, tra-la-la-la-la-la
und sollt die Ehe anders sein, dann spring
ich nicht hinein, o nein, o nein! Nein, nein,
nein, nein, nein, nein, nein, nein!

Camille, Zeta, Valencienne, Chor:
Das hat Rrrasss' so, tra-la-la-la-la-la
tra-la-la-la-la-la

Hanna:
What do you mean?

Danilo:
Fall in love often, seldom get engaged, and
never marry!
Marriage is a private matter to me, I
speak only as a diplomat, truly a point of
view that has long been out of fashion.
Marriage should always be a two-way
agreement, but soon it becomes a
triumvirate and often simply counts its
weak moments!
From the European balance of power,
when a man gets married, soon he's never
heard of again.
And the reason is usually that madam has
been given too much power for the policy
of opening doors!

Hanna:
That's outrageous!

Danilo:
Yes, I don't think I'm exaggerating but
there's something rotten in Denmark!

Hanna: *(invites all to her wedding)*
It's supposed to be a brisk matrimony :
Parisian style!
He says, "Madam;" I say: "Monsieur,"
Parisian style!
We love each other, as we understand it:
in the Parisian style!
Where everyone goes his own way:
in the Parisian style!
That's what Rrrasss' so, tra-la-la-la-la
makes it fun for me, tra-la-la-la-la
tra-la-la-la-la-la, and should the marriage be
different, then I do not jump into it, oh
no, oh no, no, no, no, no, no, no, no, no!

Camille, Zeta, Valencienne, Chorus:
This has Rrrasss' so, tra-la-la-la-la -la-
tra-la-la-la-la

Macht mir Spasss' so, tra-la-la-la-la-la
tra-la-la-la-la-la.
Und sollt die Ehe anders sein, dann
springt sie nicht hinein, o nein, o nein!

Hanna:
Dann spring ich nicht hinein, o nein, o nein.

Valencienne:
Ja, dieser Ehestand wird flott!

Hanna:
Ganz nach Pariser Art!

Valencienne:
Der Mann zieht hüt; die Frau zieht hot!

Hanna:
Ganz nach Pariser Art!

Valencienne:
Und keiner macht sich 'was daraus!

Hanna:
Ganz nach Pariser Art!

Valencienne:
Sie seh'n ganz scheidungsfähig aus.

Hanna:
Ganz nach Pariser Art!
Nein, dann spring' ich nicht hinein! Nein!

Danilo:
In mir tobt es, in mir bebt es,
in mir zuckt es, in mir juckt es!
Halt's nicht aus! Es muss heraus!
Aber nicht so wutentbrannt!
Ruhig, ruhig mit Verstand!
Zu der Vermählung, schöne Frau,
gestatten Sie eine Erzählung?

Hanna:
Gewiss, das ist ja interessant.
Seh'n Sie mich an, ich bin schon sehr
gespannt! Also, bitte!

Making fun of me, tra-la-la-la-la
tra-la-la-la-la.
And should the marriage be different,
then she does not jump in, oh no, oh no!

Hanna:
Then I will not jump in, oh no, oh no,

Valencienne:
Yes, this marriage will be lively!

Hanna:
Parisian style!

Valencienne:
The man says white, the wife says black!

Hanna:
Parisian style!

Valencienne:
And neither one thinks it's strange!

Hanna:
Parisian style!

Valencienne:
They look as if they're headed for divorce.

Hanna:
Parisian style!
No, I will not jump in! No!

Danilo:
I am agitated; I am trembling;
I am twitching; I am itching!
I can't stand it! It must be said!
But not with such burning rage!
Rather calmly, sensibly!
To your marriage, beautiful woman,
allow me to tell a story?

Hanna:
Certainly, that should be interesting.
Look at me, I'm very eager to please!
So, please!

Danilo:
Also bitte:
Es waren zwei Königskinder,
ich glaube, sie hatten sich lieb'.
Die konnten zusammen nicht kommen,
wie einst ein Dichter beschrieb.
Der Prinz, der blieb aber verschlossen,
er hatte dafür seinen Grund.

Das hat die Prinzessin verdrossen,
warum er nicht auftat den Mund.
Da hat nun die Dame Prinzessin
Getrieben ein grausames Spiel,
Sie gab ihre Hand einem Andern,
und das war dem Prinzen zu viel!

Du gnädigste Dame Prinzessin
du tätest daran gar nicht recht,
du bist auch nicht besser wie and're
vom schwachen, koketten Geschlecht!
Doch glaubst du, dass ich mich drob
kränke?
Haha! Da täuschest du dich!
Im Traume ich nicht daran denke,
das sagte der Prinz und nicht ich!
Und weiter da sagte der Prinz noch:
"Da nimm ihn, der sei dir vergönnt!"
Drauf ist er von dannen gegangen
und das tu' ich auch, Kompliment!

Hanna:
Wohin, denn Graf? Wohin?

Danilo:
Wohin? Ich? Ha!
Dort, wo ich zu Hause bin.
Ich gehe zu Maxim, dort bin ich sehr
intim, ich duze alle Damen, ruf' sie beim
Kosenamen:
Lolo, Dodo, Jou-jou, Clo-clo, Margot,
Frou-frou, sie lassen mich vergessen, was
mich so bang empfand!

Danilo:
Allein liebt er mich, nur allein!
Jetzt geht er in die Falle und...

Danilo: *(going from calm to anger)*
So please:
There were two royal children,
I think they loved each other.
They could not belong to one another,
as once a poet described.
The prince, however, remained silent,
for which he had good reason.

And the princess was upset,
as to why he did not speak.
The princess was unaware
that a merciless trick was being played,
she gave her hand to another,
and that was too much for the prince!

You gracious lady princess,
how great was the wrong that you did,
you are not better than the others,
or the feeble coquettes of your sex!
But do you think that I am heartbroken
over this?
Haha! There you are wrong!
In my dreams I do not think about it,
said the prince, but not me!
And then the prince also said:
"Take him, he must be the man for you!"
Then he disappeared, and that's exactly
what I'll do. My compliments!

Hanna:
Where to, Count? Where to?

Danilo:
Where am I going? Me? Ha!
Where I feel at home.
I go to Maxim, where I'm intimate
with all the ladies, and call them all by
their pet names:
Lolo, Dodo, Jou-Jou, Clo-Clo, Margot,
Frou-Frou, they let me forget my pain
and all my sorrows!

Hanna:
Alone he loves me, only me!
Now he's falling into my trap...

Hanna:
Das hat Rrrasss's "so, tra-la-la-la-la-la
macht mir Spass' so, tra-la-la-la-la-la.
Und sollt die Ehe anders sein,
Dann spring ich nicht hinein, o nein, o
nein, nein, nein, nein, nein, nein, nein,
nein, nein!

Hanna:
That's what Rrrass's "so, la-la-la-la
make fun of me, tra-la-la-la-la-la.
And should the marriage be different,
then I will not jump in, oh no, o no,
no, no, no, no, no, no, no, no!

Camille, Zeta, Valencienne, Chor:
Das hat Rrrasss" so, tra-la-la-la-la-la
tra-la-la-la-la-la.
Macht mir Spass' so, tra-la-la-la-la-la
tra-la-la-la-la-la.
Und sollt die Ehe anders sein, dann
springt sie nicht hinein, o nein, o nein!

Camille, Zeta, Valencienne, Chorus:
This is what Rrrasss" so, tra-la-la-la-la
tra-la-la-la -la-la.
Make fun of me, so tra-la-la-la-la tra-la-la-
la-la.
And if the marriage is different,
then she will not jump in, oh no, oh no !

End of Act II

Act III

Hanna Glawari's residence in Paris sset up as an elegant restaurant and a replica of Maxim's. Valencienne, Baron Zeta's wife, is dressed as a grisette.

Valencienne, Grisettes:
Ja, wir sind es, die Grisetten von Pariser Kabaretten!

Valencienne, Grisettes:
Yes, we are the Grisettes from Paris cabarets!

Valencienne:
Lolo! Dodo! Jou-Jou! Frou-rou! Clo-Clo! Margot! Et moi!

Valencienne: *(introducing Grisettes)*
Lolo! Dodo! Jou-Jou, Frou-Frou! Clo-Clo! Margot! And me!

Auf dem Boulevard am Abend,
trippel-trapp und trippel-trapp,
da flanieren wir Grisetten Coquettierend
auf und ab!

On the boulevard in the evening,
trippling and trippling,
there stroll we Grisettes, flirting back and forth!

Valencienne, Grisettes:
Trippel-trapp und trippel-trapp!

Valencienne, Grisettes:
Trippling, trippling, triple-trapping!

Valencienne:
Und mit Goldlackhalbstiefletten
und mit Hüten, Pschüttcoquetten,
gehen wir dort auf und ab.

Valencienne:
And with shiny gold-lacquered half-boots, and with hats, bulk suits, and hats, we parade there, back and forth there.

Valencienne, Grisettes:
Ja, so sind wir die Grisetten von Pariser Kabaretten.

Valencienne, Grisettes:
Yes, we are the Grisettes, from Parisian cabarets.

Valencienne: (again pointing to each girl)
Lolo! Dodo! Jou-Jou! Frou-Frou! Clo-Clo! Margot! Et moi!

Valencienne: *(pointing to each girl)*
Lolo! Dodo! Jou-Jou, Frou-Frou! Clo-Clo! Margot! And me!

Ritantouri tantirette,
Eh voilà les belles grisettes!
Les grisettes de Paris!

Ritantouri tantirette,
Eh there are the beautiful grisettes!
The grisettes of Paris!

Valencienne:
Wie die Spinnen in ihr Netzchen,
zippel, zippel-zapp,
sich die kleinen Falter fangen,
fangen wir die Männer, schwapp!

Valencienne:
Like the spiders in their nets,
zippel, zippel-zapp,
Catch the little butterflies,
we catch the men, snap!

Valencienne, Grisettes:
Zippel, zippel, zippel-zapp!

Valencienne, Grisettes:
Zippel, zippel, zippel-zapp!

Valencienne:
Lassen sie gern zippeln zappeln,
Trippel-trippel trippel-trapp!
Und dann geh'n wir wieder weiter
Coquettierend auf und ab!

Valencienne:
Then we turn them loose again, now,
Trippel-trippel trippel-trapp!
And then we will go on again, coquett-
ishly flirting back and forth!

Valencienne, Grisettes:
Ja, so sind wir, die Grisetten, von Pariser
Kabaretten!

Valencienne, Grisettes:
Yes, that's how we are, the Grisettes
from Parisian cabarets!

Hanna teases Danilo about inviting grisettes to make him feel at home.
Danilo forbids Hanna to marry Camille. Hanna responds: "Because you love me?"
Danilo laughs it off and Hanna agrees not to marry Camille.
Danilo inquires about Hanna's rendezvous with Camille in the pavilion.
She confesses that it was not her, but another lady. Finally, Hanna's patience ends
and she tells him to stop pretending — just tell her that he loves her.

Danilo looks at Hanna longingly, and after struggling with his feelings,
he sings to her.

Danilo:
Lippen schweigen, 's flüstern Geigen:
hab mich lieb!
All' die Schritte sagen bitte, hab mich lieb!
Jeder Druck der Hände deutlich mir's
beschrieb. Er sagt klar, 's ist wahr, 's ist
wahr, du hast mich lieb!

Danilo:
Lips are silent, violins whisper:
Love me!
Every step says, please love me!
Every clasp of hands clearly showed me.
It's true, it's true,
you love me! You love me!

Hanna:
Warum? Why?
Bei jedem Walzerschnitt tanzt auch die
Seele mit,
da hüpft das Herzchen klein,
es klopft und pocht: Sei mein! Sei mein!
Und der Mund, der spricht kein Wort,
doch tönt es fort und immerfort:

Ich hab' dich ja so lieb, ich hab' dich lieb!

Hanna:
Why? Why?
At each waltz step, the soul will dance
along,
then the little heart pounds, knocks and
pounds: Be mine! Be mine!
And the mouth speaks not a word,
but echoes its sounds on and on:
(looking at each other)
I love you so much, I love you so!

Danilo announces that Hanna is not marrying Camille. Valencienne is relieved.
Danilo lets it be known that the lady in the pavilon was not Hanna, but another lady.
Zeta inquires who that might have been. Njegus enters with a fan in his hand and
announces that he found it in the pavilion. Valencienne, after a shudder, show the
fan to her husband Zeta and asks him to read what is witte on it:
Zeta reads: "I am a respectable wife."

Hanna, Herrenchor:
Ja, das Studium der Weiber ist schwer.
Ach, die Weiber, diese Weiber!

Zeta:
Nimmt uns Männer verteufelt auch her!

Danilo:
Niemals kennt doch an Seele und Leib
Man das Weib.

Alles:
Weib, Weib, Weib, Weib!
Mädchen zart, Gretchenart, blondes Haar,
mit dem treuesten Blauäugleinpaar.

Herrenchor:'
Ob sie schwarz oder rot oder blond sind
gefärbt s'ist egal, man wird doch gegärbt.

Frauenchor:
Ob wir schwarz oder rot oder blond sind
gefärbt, s'ist egal, er wird doch gegärbt.

Hanna, Men's Chorus:
Yes, the study of the women is difficult.
Oh, the women, these women!

Zeta:
It's getting us men bedeviled!

Danilo:
One can never quite grasp the soul and
body of woman.

All:
Wife, wife, wife, wife! Woman, woman,
Tender maiden, Gretel-like, blond hair,
with the most innocent pair of blue-eyes.

Men's Chorus:
Whether her hair is dyed black or red or
blond, we are still smitten.

Women's Chorus:
Whether their hair is dyed black or red
or blond are dyed, we wind up smitten.

End of Operetta

DICTIONARY OF OPERA AND MUSICAL TERMS

Accelerando - Play the music faster, but gradually.

Adagio - At slow or gliding tempo, not as slow as Largo, but not as fast as Andante.

Agitato - Restless or agitated.

Allegro - At a brisk or lively tempo, faster than Andante but not as fast as Presto.

Andante - A moderately slow, easy-going tempo.

Appoggiatura - An extra or embellishing note preceding a main melodic note or tone. Usually written as a note of smaller size, it shares the time value of the main note.

Arabesque - Flourishes or fancy patterns usually applying to vocal virtuosity.

Aria - A solo song usually structured in a formal pattern. Arias generally convey reflective and introspective thoughts rather than descriptive action.

Arietta - A shortened form of aria.

Arioso - A musical passage or composition having a mixture of free recitative and metrical song.

Arpeggio - Producing the tones of a chord in succession but not simultaneously.

Atonal - Music that is not anchored in traditional musical tonality; it uses the chromatic scale impartially, does not use the diatonic scale and has no keynote or tonal center.

Ballad Opera - 18th century English opera consisting of spoken dialogue and music derived from popular ballad and folksong sources. The most famous is *The Beggar's Opera* which was a satire of the Italian opera seria.

Bar - A vertical line across the stave that divides the music into units.

Baritone - A male singing voice ranging between the bass and tenor.

Baroque - A style of artistic expression prevalent in the 17th century that is marked generally by the use of complex forms, bold ornamentation, and florid decoration. The Baroque period extends from approximately 1600 to 1750 and includes the works of the original creators of modern opera, the Camerata, as well as the later works by Bach and Handel.

Bass - The lowest male voices, usually divided into categories such as:

> **Basso buffo** - A bass voice that specializes in comic roles like Dr. Bartolo in Rossini's *The Barber of Seville*.

> **Basso cantante** - A bass voice that demonstrates melodic singing quality rather than comic or tragic: King Philip in Verdi's *Don Carlos*.

> **Basso profundo** - the deepest, most profound, or most dramatic of bass voices: Sarastro in Mozart's *The Magic Flute.*

Bel canto - Literally "beautiful singing." It originated in Italian opera of the 17th and 18th centuries and stressed beautiful tones produced with ease, clarity, purity, evenness, together with an agile vocal technique and virtuosity. Bel canto flourished in the first half of the 19th century in the works of Rossini, Bellini, and Donizetti.

Cabaletta - Typically a lively bravura extension of an aria or duet that creates a climax. The term is derived from the Italian word "cavallo," or horse: it metaphorically describes a horse galloping to the finish line.

Cadenza - A flourish or brilliant part of an aria commonly inserted just before a finale.

Camerata - A gathering of Florentine writers and musicians between 1590 and 1600 who attempted to recreate what they believed was the ancient Greek theatrical synthesis of drama, music, and stage spectacle; their experimentation led to the creation of the early structural forms of modern opera.

Cantabile - An expression indication urging the singer to sing sweetly.

Cantata - A choral piece generally containing Scriptural narrative texts: Bach Cantatas.

Cantilena - A lyrical melodic line meant to be played or sung "cantabile," or with sweetness and expression.

Canzone - A short, lyrical operatic song usually containing no narrative association with the drama but rather simply reflecting the character's state of mind: Cherubino's "Voi che sapete" in Mozart's *The Marriage of Figaro.* Shorter versions are called canzonettas.

Castrato - A young male singer who was surgically castrated to retain his treble voice.

Cavatina - A short aria popular in the 18th century without the da capo repeat section.

Classical Period - The period between the Baroque and Romantic periods. The Classical period is generally considered to have begun with the birth of Mozart (1756) and ended with Beethoven's death (1830). Stylistically, the music of the period stressed clarity, precision, and rigid structural forms.

Coda - A trailer or tailpiece added on by the composer after the music's natural conclusion.

Coloratura - Literally colored: it refers to a soprano singing in the bel canto tradition with great agility, virtuosity, embellishments and ornamentation: Joan Sutherland singing in Donizetti's *Lucia di Lammermoor.*

Commedia dell'arte - A popular form of dramatic presentation originating in Renaissance Italy in which highly stylized characters were involved in comic plots involving mistaken identities and misunderstandings. The standard characters were Harlequin and Colombine: The "play within a play" in Leoncavallo's *I Pagliacci.*

Comprimario - A singer portraying secondary character roles such as confidantes, servants, and messengers.

Continuo - A bass part (as for a keyboard or stringed instrument) that was used especially in baroque ensemble music; it consists of a succession of bass notes with figures that indicate the required chords. Also called *figured bass, thoroughbass.*

Contralto - The lowest female voice derived from "contra" against, and "alto" voice, a voice between the tenor and mezzo-soprano.

Countertenor, or male alto vocal range - A high male voice generally singing within the female high soprano ranges.

Counterpoint - The combination of one or more independent melodies added into a single harmonic texture in which each retains its linear character: polyphony. The most sophisticated form of counterpoint is the fugue form in which up to 6 to 8 voices are combined, each providing a variation on the basic theme but each retaining its relation to the whole.

Crescendo - A gradual increase in the volume of a musical passage.

Da capo - Literally "from the top": repeat. Early 17th century da capo arias were in the form of A B A, the last A section repeating the first A section.

Deus ex machina - Literally "god out of a machine." A dramatic technique in which a person or thing appears or is introduced suddenly and unexpectedly; it provides a contrived solution to an apparently insoluble dramatic difficulty.

Diatonic - Relating to a major or minor musical scale that comprises intervals of five whole steps and two half steps.

Diminuendo - Gradually getting softer, the opposite of crescendo.

Dissonance - A mingling of discordant sounds that do not harmonize within the diatonic scale.

Diva - Literally a "goddess"; generally refers to a female opera star who either possesses, or pretends to possess, great rank.

Dominant - The fifth tone of the diatonic scale: in the key of C, the dominant is G.

Dramma giocoso - Literally meaning amusing, or lighthearted. Like tragicomedy it represents an opera whose story combines both serious and comic elements: Mozart's _Don Giovanni._

Falsetto - Literally a lighter or "false" voice; an artificially produced high singing voice that extends above the range of the full voice.

Fioritura - Literally "flower"; a flowering ornamentation or embellishment of the vocal line within an aria.

Forte, Fortissimo - Forte (_f_) means loud: mezzo forte (_mf_) is fairly loud; fortissimo (_ff_) even louder, and additional _fff_'s indicate greater degrees of loudness.

Glissando - A rapid sliding up or down the scale.

Grand Opera - An opera in which there is no spoken dialogue and the entire text is set to music, frequently treating serious and dramatic subjects. Grand Opera flourished in France in the 19th century (Meyerbeer) and most notably by Verdi (Aida): the genre is epic in scale and combines spectacle, large choruses, scenery, and huge orchestras.

Heldentenor - A tenor with a powerful dramatic voice who possesses brilliant top notes and vocal stamina. Heldentenors are well suited to heroic (Wagnerian) roles: Lauritz Melchoir in Wagner's _Tristan und Isolde_.

Imbroglio - Literally "Intrigue"; an operatic scene with chaos and confusion and appropriate diverse melodies and rhythms.

Largo or larghetto - Largo indicates a very slow tempo; Larghetto is slightly faster than Largo.

Legato - Literally "tied"; therefore, successive tones that are connected smoothly. Opposing Legato would be Marcato (strongly accented and punctuated) and Staccato (short and aggressive).

Leitmotif - A short musical passage attached to a person, thing, feeling, or idea that provides associations when it recurs or is recalled.

Libretto - Literally "little book"; the text of an opera. On Broadway, the text of songs is called "lyrics" but the spoken text in the play is called the "book."

Lied - A German song; the plural is "lieder." Originally German art songs of the 19th century.

Light opera, or operetta - Operas that contain comic elements but light romantic plots: Johann Strauss's *Die Fledermaus.*

Maestro - From the Italian "master": a term of respect to conductors, composers, directors, and great musicians.

Melodrama - Words spoken over music. Melodrama appears in Beethoven's *Fidelio* but flourished during the late 19th century in the operas of Massenet (*Manon*). Melodrama should not be confused with melodrama when it describes a work that is characterized by extravagant theatricality and by the predominance of plot and physical action over characterization.

Mezza voce - Literally "medium voice," or singing with medium or half volume; it is generally intended as a vocal means to intensify emotion.

Mezzo-soprano - A woman's voice with a range between that of the soprano and contralto.

Molto - Very. Molto agitato means very agitated.

Obbligato - An elaborate accompaniment to a solo or principal melody that is usually played by a single instrument.

Octave - A musical interval embracing eight diatonic degrees: therefore, from C to C is an octave.

Opera - Literally "a work"; a dramatic or comic play combining music.

Opera buffa - Italian comic opera that flourished during the bel canto era. Buffo characters were usually basses singing patter songs: Dr. Bartolo in Rossini's *The Barber of Seville,* and Dr. Dulcamara in Donizetti's *The Elixir of Love.*

Opéra comique - A French opera characterized by spoken dialogue interspersed between the arias and ensemble numbers, as opposed to Grand Opera in which there is no spoken dialogue.

Operetta, or light opera - Operas that contain comic elements but tend to be more romantic: Strauss's *Die Fledermaus,* Offenbach's *La Périchole*, and Lehar's *The Merry Widow*. In operettas, there is usually much spoken dialogue, dancing, practical jokes, and mistaken identities.

Oratorio - A lengthy choral work, usually of a religious or philosophical nature and consisting chiefly of recitatives, arias, and choruses but in deference to its content, performed without action or scenery: Handel's *Messiah.*

Ornamentation - Extra embellishing notes—appoggiaturas, trills, roulades, or cadenzas—that enhance a melodic line.

Overture - The orchestral introduction to a musical dramatic work that frequently incorporates musical themes within the work.

Parlando - Literally "speaking"; the imitation of speech while singing, or singing that is almost speaking over the music. It is usually short and with minimal orchestral accompaniment.

Patter - Words rapidly and quickly delivered. Figaro's Largo in Rossini's *The Barber of Seville* is a patter song.

Pentatonic - A five-note scale, like the black notes within an octave on the piano.

Piano - Soft volume.

Pitch - The property of a musical tone that is determined by the frequency of the waves producing it.

Pizzicato - A passage played by plucking the strings instead of stroking the string with the bow.

Polyphony - Literally "many voices." A style of musical composition in which two or more independent melodies are juxtaposed in harmony; counterpoint.

Polytonal - The use of several tonal schemes simultaneously.

Portamento - A continuous gliding movement from one tone to another.

Prelude - An orchestral introduction to an act or the whole opera. An Overture can appear only at the beginning of an opera.

Presto, Prestissimo - Very fast and vigorous.

Prima Donna - The female star of an opera cast. Although the term was initially used to differentiate between the dramatic and vocal importance of a singer, today it generally describes the personality of a singer rather than her importance in the particular opera.

Prologue - A piece sung before the curtain goes up on the opera proper: Tonio's Prologue in Leoncavallo's *I Pagliacci*.

Quaver - An eighth note.

Range - The divisions of the voice: soprano, mezzo-soprano, contralto, tenor, baritone, and bass.

Recitative - A formal device that that advances the plot. It is usually a rhythmically free vocal style that imitates the natural inflections of speech; it represents the dialogue and narrative in operas and oratorios. Secco recitative is accompanied by harpsichord and sometimes with cello or continuo instruments and *accompagnato* indicates that the recitative is accompanied by the orchestra.

Ritornello - A short recurrent instrumental passage between elements of a vocal composition.

Romanza - A solo song that is usually sentimental; it is usually shorter and less complex than an aria and rarely deals with terror, rage, and anger.

Romantic Period - The period generally beginning with the raiding of the Bastille (1789) and the last revolutions and uprisings in Europe (1848). Romanticists generally found inspiration in nature and man. Beethoven's *Fidelio* (1805) is considered the first Romantic opera, followed by the works of Verdi and Wagner.

Roulade - A florid vocal embellishment sung to one syllable.

Rubato - Literally "robbed"; it is a fluctuation of tempo within a musical phrase, often against a rhythmically steady accompaniment.

Secco - The accompaniment for recitative played by the harpsichord and sometimes continuo instruments.

Semitone - A half-step, the smallest distance between two notes. In the key of C, the notes are E and F, and B and C.

Serial music - Music based on a series of tones in a chosen pattern without regard for traditional tonality.

Sforzando - Sudden loudness and force; it must stick out from the texture and provide a shock.

Singspiel - Early German musical drama employing spoken dialogue between songs: Mozart's *The Magic Flute*.

Soprano - The highest range of the female voice ranging from lyric (light and graceful quality) to dramatic (fuller and heavier in tone).

Sotto voce - Literally "below the voice"; sung softly between a whisper and a quiet conversational tone.

Soubrette - A soprano who sings supporting roles in comic opera: Adele in Strauss's *Die Fledermaus*, or Despina in Mozart's *Così fan tutte.*

Spinto - From the Italian "spingere" (to push); a soprano having lyric vocal qualities who "pushes" the voice to achieve heavier dramatic qualities.

Sprechstimme - Literally "speak voice." The singer half sings a note and half speaks; the declamation sounds like speaking but the duration of pitch makes it seem almost like singing.

Staccato - Short, clipped, rapid articulation; the opposite of the caressing effects of legato.

Stretto - A concluding passage performed in a quicker tempo to create a musical climax.

Strophe - Music repeated for each verse of an aria.

Syncopation - Shifting the beat forward or back from its usual place in the bar; it is a temporary displacement of the regular metrical accent in music caused typically by stressing the weak beat.

Supernumerary - A "super"; a performer with a non-singing role: "Spear-carrier."

Tempo - Time, or speed. The ranges are Largo for very slow to Presto for very fast.

Tenor - Highest natural male voice.

Tessitura - The general range of a melody or voice part; but specifically, the part of the register in which most of the tones of a melody or voice part lie.

Tonality - The organization of all the tones and harmonies of a piece of music in relation to a tonic (the first tone of its scale).

Tone Poem - An orchestral piece with a program; a script.

Tonic - The keynote of the key in which a piece is written. C is the tonic of C major.

Trill - Two adjacent notes rapidly and repeatedly alternated.

Tutti - All together.

Twelve tone - The 12 chromatic tones of the octave placed in a chosen fixed order and constituting with some permitted permutations and derivations the melodic and harmonic material of a serial musical piece. Each note of the chromatic scale is used as part of the melody before any other note gets repeated.

Verismo - Literally "truth"; the artistic use of contemporary everyday material in preference to the heroic or legendary in opera. A movement from the late 19th century: *Carmen.*

Vibrato - A "vibration"; a slightly tremulous effect imparted to vocal or instrumental tone for added warmth and expressiveness by slight and rapid variations in pitch.

Opera Journeys™ Mini Guide Series

Opera Journeys™ Libretto Series

Opera Classics Library™ Series

A History of Opera: Milestones and Metamorphoses

Puccini Companion

Verdi Companion

Mozart's Da Ponte Operas

Fifty Timeless Classics

PUCCINI COMPANION

Hard or Soft Cover editions

COMPLETE LIBRETTOS
Italian-English side-by-side

STORY NARRATIVE
with 100s of Music Highlight Examples

ANALYSIS AND COMMENTARY

Print or Ebook

A HISTORY of OPERA; MILESTONES and MEAMORPHOSES

432 pages, soft cover / 21 chapters
0ver 250 music examples
featuring
• A comprehensive survey of milestones in opera history
• All periods are analyzed in depth:
Baroque, Classical, Romantic, Bel Canto, Opera Buffa,
German Romanticism, Wagner, music drama, Verismo,
plus analyses "Tristan Chord," atonalism, minimalism.

Print or Ebook

OPERA JOURNEYS' COLLECTION: 50 TIMELESS OPERA CLASSICS

816-page Soft Cover volume
*A collection of fifty of the most popular operas
in the Opera Journeys Mini Guide Series,
each: Story Narrative and 100s of Music Examples,*
PLUS insightful, in delpth Commentary and Analysis

Print ot Ebook

MOZART'S DA PONTE OPERAS
DON GIOVANNI; MARRIAGE FIGARO; COSI FAN TUTTE

348-page Soft or Hard Cover Edition

*Mozart: Master of Musical Characterization;
Da Ponte: Ambassador of Italian Culture.*
*Featuring: Principal Characters, Brief Story Synopsis,
Story Narrative, Music Highlight Examples,
insightful in depth Commentary and Analysis,
Librettos with Italian-English translations side-by-side*

ORDER: Opera Journeys' Web Site www.operajourneys.com

OPERA JOURNEYS LIBRETTO SERIES

Print or Ebook

New translations (side-by-side) with Music Highlight Examples

•Aida •The Barber of Seville •La Bohème
•Carmen •Cavalleria Rusticana •La Cenerentola
•Così fan tutte •Don Carlo •Don Giovanni
•La Fanciulla del West •Gianni Schicchi
•Lucia di Lammermoor •Madama Butterfly
•The Magic Flute •Manon Lescaut
•The Marriage of Figaro •A Masked Ball
•Otello •I Pagliacci •Rigoletto •La Rondine
•Salome Samson and Delilah •Suor Angelica
•Il Tabarro •Tosca •La Traviata •Il Trovatore •Turandot

OPERA JOURNEYS MINI GUIDE SERIES

Print or Ebook

featuring 125 titles

• *Brief Story Synopsis*

• *Principal Characters*

• *Story Narrative*

• *Music Highlight Examples*

• *Commentary and Analysis*

•The Abduction from the Seraglio •Adriana Lecouvreur •L'Africaine •Aida •Andrea Chénier
•Anna Bolena •Ariadne auf Naxos •Armida •Attila •The Ballad of Baby Doe •The Barber of Seville
•Duke Bluebeard's Castle •La Bohème •Boris Godunov •Candide •Capriccio •Carmen
•Cavalleria Rusticana •Cendrillon •La Cenerentola •La Clemenza di Tito •Le Comte Ory
•Così fan tutte •The Crucible •La Damnation de Faust •The Death of Klinghoffer •Doctor Atomic
Don Carlo • Don Giovanni •Don Pasquale •La Donna del Lago •The Elixir of Love •Elektra •Ernani
•Eugene Onegin •Falstaff •La Fanciulla del West •Faust •La Fille du Régiment
•Fidelio •Die Fledermaus •The Flying Dutchman •Die Frau ohne Schatten
•Der Freischütz •Gianni Schicchi •La Gioconda •Hamlet •Hansel and Gretel •Henry VIII
•Iolanta •L'Italiana in Algeri •Les Huguenots •Iphigénie en Tauride •Julius Caesar •Lakmé
•Lohengrin •Lucia di Lammermoor •Macbeth •Madama Butterfly •The Magic Flute
•The Makropolis Case •Manon •Manon Lescaut •Maria Stuarda •The Marriage of Figaro
•A Masked Ball •Die Meistersinger •The Mikado •Nabucco •Nixon in China •Norma
•Of Mice and Men •Orfeo ed Euridice •Otello •I Pagliacci •Parsifal •The Pearl Fishers
•Pelléas et Mélisande •Porgy and Bess •Prince Igor •I Puritani •The Queen of Spades
•The Rake's Progress •The Rape of Lucretia •The Rhinegold •Rigoletto •The Ring of the Nibelung
•Roberto Devereaux •Rodalinda •Roméo et Juliette •La Rondine •Der Rosenkavalier •Rusalka
•Salome •Samson and Delilah •Show Boat •Siegfried •Simon Boccanegra •La Sonnambula
•Suor Angelica •Susannah •Il Tabarro •The Tales of Hoffmann •Tannhäuser •Thaïs •Tosca
•La Traviata •Tristan and Isolde •Il Trittico •Les Troyens •Il Trovatore •Turandot
•Twilight of the Gods •The Valkyrie •Werther •West Side Story •Wozzeck

OPERA CLASSICS LIBRARY™

Opera Study Guides

WITH

Librettos

EDITED BY Burton D. Fisher

Available at
Amazon.com or Opera Journeys.com

Each *Opera Classic Library* edition features...

- *Principal Characters in the Opera*
- *Brief Story Synopsis*
- *Commentary and Analysis*
- *Story Narrative with Music Highlights*
- *Libretto - parallel, side-by-side translation*

"THE COLLECTION"

Made in the USA
Las Vegas, NV
03 November 2021